THE FUTURE OF
THE FIRST AMENDMENT

THE FUTURE OF THE FIRST AMENDMENT

The Digital Media, Civic Education, and Free Expression Rights in America's High Schools

Kenneth Dautrich,
David A. Yalof,
and
Mark Hugo López

ROWMAN & LITTLEFIELD PUBLISHERS, INC.
Lanham • Boulder • New York • Toronto • Plymouth, UK

KH

ROWMAN & LITTLEFIELD PUBLISHERS, INC.

Published in the United States of America
by Rowman & Littlefield Publishers, Inc.
A wholly owned subsidary of The Rowman & Littlefield Publishing Group, Inc.
4501 Forbes Boulevard, Suite 200, Lanham, Maryland 20706
www.rowmanlittlefield.com

Estover Road
Plymouth PL6 7PY
United Kingdom

British Library Cataloguing in Publication Information Available

Library of Congress Cataloging-in-Publication Data:

Dautrich, Kenneth.
 The future of the First Amendment : the digital media, civic education, and free
expression rights in America's high schools / Kenneth Dautrich, David A. Yalof, and Mark
Hugo López.
    p. cm.
 Includes bibliographical references.
 ISBN-13: 978-0-7425-6282-0 (cloth : alk. paper)
 ISBN-10: 0-7425-6282-4 (cloth : alk. paper)
 1. United States. Constitution. 1st Amendment. 2. Freedom of speech—United States. 3.
Freedom of the press—United States. 4. High school students—United States. 5. Student
publications—United States. 6. Digital media—United States. 7. Freedom of speech—
Study and teaching—United States. I. Yalof, David Alistair. II. López, Mark Hugo, 1967–
III. Title.
 KF4770.D38 2008
 342.7308'53—dc22   2008001508

Printed in the United States of America

∞™ The paper used in this publication meets the minimum requirements of American
National Standard for Information Sciences—Permanence of Paper for Printed Library
Materials, ANSI/NISO Z39.48-1992.

8/28/09

To the next generation of Americans,
on whom the future of our democratic system rests

Contents

Preface

FINDINGS FROM A JOHN S. AND JAMES L. KNIGHT FOUNDATION–sponsored study released in early 2005 served as a wake-up call to those interested in preserving the future of free expression rights in America. The study of 114,000 high school students documented the overwhelming lack of appreciation for free expression rights that is prevalent among the nation's high school students. It also raised serious questions about the vitality those rights have maintained among the generation that will soon be maturing into adulthood. These sobering findings led the Knight Foundation to develop and enhance a number of initiatives and programs aimed at improving the prospects for the future of the First Amendment in America. One such initiative featured increased efforts at research to examine how the educational system might effectively use the high school curriculum to improve student support for free expression rights. The research presented in this book combines findings from that original study with subsequent research that is a product of this ambitious new research program.

In *The Future of the First Amendment*, we identify a number of important connections and relationships that education reformers should consider as they seek to raise the status of the First Amendment among the nation's youth. The data point to a simple, yet important, premise: education makes a difference. Those high school students who take classes with First Amendment content tend to be more supportive of free expression rights than those who don't. Similarly, those who participate in student newspapers are more likely to support the exercise of free expression rights.

This book also investigates the digital media's role in the educational process. The digital media revolution has had a profound effect on American society, significantly influencing how citizens are able to exercise their free expression rights. Indeed, the most prevalent adopters of digital media technology (those who regularly publish opinions on their own Internet blogs) are young people. This raises an important question: does the use of these new media help to shape those users' understanding of and appreciation for freedom of expression? And if so, how can our educational system harness this dynamic to improve student support for the First Amendment?

The Future of the First Amendment documents and explores the ramifications of First Amendment education and student media activities (traditional and digital) on student support for free expression rights. Linking these curricular and extracurricular experiences to the next generation's support for free expression rights, we hope to provide guidance to educators and policy makers on methods for improving the next generation's appreciation for rights that are so central to the health of American democracy.

Acknowledgments

MANY PEOPLE CONTRIBUTED IN WAYS LARGE AND SMALL to the research that served as the basis for this book, as well as to the writing of the book itself. Certainly, none of this would have been possible without the generosity of the John S. and James L. Knight Foundation. The foundation's dedication to the value of free expression rights has produced an impressive array of programs intended to enhance the viability of the First Amendment in American society. Knight's tireless efforts to increase student support for the First Amendment represent an important contribution to the well-being of American democracy. This book may well serve as yet another weapon in Knight's arsenal to advance free expression rights. A handful of individuals at Knight not only made this research possible but also share in the intellectual capital driving our focus. Everything begins with Eric Newton who has consistently led the charge to improve the future of the First Amendment; his ideas and insights have contributed greatly to our research. Also at Knight, Julie Tarr, Denise Tom, and Bud Meyer have been extra supportive. All were a pleasure to work with at every stage of this process.

We would also like to thank Warren Watson at Ball State's J-Ideas program. Warren and his staff clearly share Knight's passion for the First Amendment. They have been associated with our program of research since day one, and our scholarship has been refined in a positive way thanks to their efforts.

In presenting various aspects of the Knight research, many other individuals have provided ideas and comments that helped us develop this book. Gene Policinski of the First Amendment Center, which also supports our annual State of the First Amendment survey (discussed in chapter 1 of this book), has been enormously helpful in every way. Countless others from organizations committed to the future of the First Amendment have helped as well, including those from the Freedom Forum, Radio and Television News Directors Association (RTNDA), American Society of Newspaper Editors (ASNE), The Center for Information and Research on Civic Learning and Engagement (CIRCLE), Quill & Scroll, the Student Press Law Center, and the Journalism Educators Association (JEA). We only wish we could name all of them here. This was as much a labor of love for them as it was for us.

Introduction

A STUDY OF AMERICAN HIGH SCHOOL STUDENTS released by the John S. and James L. Knight Foundation in 2005 found alarmingly high levels of ignorance, lethargy, and agnosticism toward the very rights that underlie the most basic tenets of American democracy. Nearly half of America's youth either supported, or were unsure if they would support, the government's right to require approval of a news story before its publication. Almost three-quarters of students either didn't know how they felt about the First Amendment or openly admitted that they take it for granted. Three-quarters erroneously reported thinking that flag burning was an illegal activity, and one-third felt that the First Amendment goes too far in the rights it guarantees.

These and a host of other eye-opening findings from the Knight study underscored an important national discussion over the next generation's understanding of and appreciation for free expression rights. Free expression, as well as the value placed on it, has been central to the development of the American nation. It serves to watchdog government and corporate corruption; it facilitates debate on political issues and informs voters; it provides for variety and diversity of thought to keep the intellectual, artistic, and scientific minds of the nation sharp. It promotes a free marketplace of ideas, where the best and brightest compete for majority support and public acclaim. If American stock in free expression helped create and sustain what has become the world's most powerful nation, to what extent is the future of American democracy at risk if today's high school students are so uninformed about and unappreciative of free expression rights? If the future generation of Americans, today's high school generation, largely undervalues the significance of free expression rights, what can we expect about the future vitality of those rights? Will this undervaluation make it easier for government in future years to encroach on and limit expression that it disagrees with? Will the supply of ideas in the "marketplace of ideas" shrink, thereby rendering America a lesser society than it has been?

Ultimately, the health of democracy is in the hands of the American people. As Abraham Lincoln once admonished about America, "Public sentiment is everything. With public sentiment, nothing can fail; without it, nothing can succeed."[1] The things that Americans care about and value help them make choices about leadership, and elected leaders are sensitive to the will of the people. And so, while the words of the First Amendment provide a brilliant legal articulation of free expression rights, the real protection of those rights is found in the hearts and minds of the American polity. As Judge Learned Hand once said,

> I often wonder whether we do not rest our hopes too much upon constitutions, upon laws, and upon courts. These are false hopes; believe me, these are false hopes. Liberty lies in the hearts of men and women; when it dies there, no constitution, no law, no court can save it.[2]

It is in this spirit that we seek to study and assess the state of the free expression rights in America's high schools, frame it within larger debates over the nature of the digital media revolution, and identify some possible ways of improving future generations' appreciation and support for those rights in American society.

This book takes up the question of what can be done to improve the future of free expression rights in America by instilling in future generations an understanding of the important role that those rights play in enhancing and sustaining democratic governance. Like members of any society, Americans develop their political values through a process known as "political socialization." Free speech and free press have been an important part of American culture for more than two centuries. They are written in the First Amendment, and they are celebrated as not only a positive characteristic of American society but also as means of sustaining the American brand of democracy. Free expression values, which promote both the free and open press and the marketplace of ideas, have been transferred from generation to generation by a variety of forces. The factors bearing on the political socialization process, known as "agents" of socialization, are many and varied. They include families, peer groups, and religious organizations. All of these agents play a role in transferring important political values, such as free expression rights, from one generation to the next. In this book, we specifically examine the role that two other agents of political socialization play in promoting an appreciation for free expression: secondary education and the mass media.

While it is important to examine all of the factors that might improve the future status of free expression, we focus on these two in particular for a few important reasons. First, an important goal of American education, particularly free public education, is to promote the development of an informed citizenry ready and able to function productively as democratic citizens. The American nation was founded on a set of principles that promote citizen participation in the political system. The better educated and more informed the public, the higher will be quality of government performance. Since its establishment, a primary goal of free public education has been to enhance the capacity of future generations to take part in the political system.[3] Thus, in this book we specifically examine the role of the nation's secondary schools in engendering an appreciation and affinity for the free expression rights that are so central to American political culture.

Second, we focus on the role of the media not only because the media represent a powerful source of information to citizens but also because the media play a role in transferring political values. Americans of all ages use the modern media as their primary source of information, and much of what they learn about the political system comes from the media. Even more significantly, the mass media are a primary vehicle through which free expression rights are exercised. The provision of information and commentary through traditional media sources, such as newspapers, radio, magazines, and television, enable the mass circulation of ideas and opinions. The so-called digital media that have emerged over the past decade or two facilitate even more Americans' use of their free expression rights. Blogging, posting information on Web pages, and even e-mailing now allow individual citizens to become their own publishers. More than ever, information, ideas, and opinions can be expressed and made available to mass audiences, significantly enhancing the supply of ideas in the marketplace.

The strong propensity of young people to make use of these new technologies further suggests that the media, as an agent of socialization, must be scrutinized. While social scientists often refer to the generation of students born between 1982 and 2000 as "Millennials,"[4] historians are more likely to remember its members by the electronic devices and the technology they use; perhaps it's more accurate to think of these teens as the "MP3" generation, the "iPod" generation, or even the "BlackBerry" generation. What is the nature of this new technology that has captured the attention of this generation in particular, and does it influence both their understanding and use of free expression rights?

Third, the nexus of issues between the institutions of secondary education and the media are significant. Schools teach students to use media and digital media technologies. Many schools offer instruction in journalism and the role of the media in society. Many schools also offer instruction in free expression rights (through civics and American government classes) and attempt to promote free expression through school student media activities, such as a school newspaper. Along with curricular and extracurricular treatment of the media in the schools, schools are addressing a number of emerging problems related to the media. These include issues surrounding the regulation of social-networking sites, which set the stage for a broader discussion of the state of press freedoms in the nation's high schools.

Students posting news and information on social-networking sites are not just acting as reporters: they are their own editors and self-publishers. Principals are not in a position to censor students' material prior to its publication on the Internet (although they may try to punish students for material they have posted after the fact). Essentially, the freedom of the press no longer frames negotiations between students, their teachers, and the principals; students may apply these First Amendment freedoms on their own. This book attempts to explore this new learning paradigm of "student as editor/publisher" in the context of secondary education. Surrounded by pressures to focus on reading, writing and mathematics exclusively (the push for standardized scores, No Child Left Behind legislation, etc.) and faced with tightening budgets that have led school officials to encourage the proliferation of Internet publications, student online communications were destined to find a home outside the reach of school officials. Social networking sites filled that need with unimaginable success.

The tentative status of free expression rights, as measured through the Knight Foundation's surveys of American high school students, raises a serious flag about the future vitality of these rights. It suggests that we should look for ways to enhance future generations' understanding of and appreciation for how freedom of speech and freedom of the press play a pivotal role in promoting a healthy democracy. Given the relevant ways in which secondary education and the mass media relate to the promotion of free expression, this book attempts to do just that. By studying the attitudes and experiences of students, high school teachers, and high schools principals, we explore the role of the nations' high schools in socializing students toward the value of free expression. We also examine the role of the media, particularly the "digital media," in developing these values. What are the schools doing that works? What are they doing that doesn't? How can schools channel the potential of the Internet toward a more productive appreciation for free expression, as well as inspire greater utilization of free expression rights? Policy makers and educational reformers are now seeking ways to enhance civic engagement and civic education to reinvigorate the next generation and prepare them for a productive life in democratic governance.

Organization of This Book

This book provides an examination of the impact of secondary education and the media on student attitudes about free expression rights and suggests policy changes that might improve the value and vibrancy of free expression in the future. The book is organized to accomplish this in the following way.

In chapter 1 we explore data gathered through a grant from the John S. and James L. Knight Foundation in 2004 and 2006 regarding student knowledge of and attitudes about the First Amendment and free expression rights in particular. We compare these findings to adult survey results drawn from the First Amendment Center's yearly State of the First Amendment surveys dating back to 1997. What are student orientations toward free speech and free press rights, and how do they compare to adult orientations? Do students appreciate these free expression rights to the same degree that adults do? Is future support for the First Amendment in danger?

In chapter 2 we examine the role of the educational system in teaching First Amendment rights and other constitutional rules to students and place the current state of cybercommunications into this context. We also examine the legal environment that schools must work within as they consider the use of free expression rights by students. What is the nature of political socialization, and what role do public schools in particular play in promoting democracy and teaching citizenship? We also look at recent data on the state of First Amendment education in the schools. Opinions of students, teachers, and even school principals will all be considered in this framework.

In chapter 3, we specifically examine the relationship between free expression rights, media, and journalism education in the high school curriculum and related student attitudes. We also look at the relationship between extracurricular student media experiences (e.g., working on the school newspaper) and attitudes about free expression rights. This chapter seeks to determine if, and the extent to which, the high school curriculum and student media offerings help promote positive student orientations toward free expression in our society, controlling for a rich set of potentially confounding factors.

Chapter 4 explores the digital media revolution in much greater depth. How does the use of digital media affect the exercise of free expression by students in general? Do students' orientations toward the new and old media affect the way they perceive press freedoms? In chapter 5, we analyze the relationship between the use of new media on attitudes about free expression rights. Many students across all demographic groups in our society now use the Internet to get news and information through a variety of sources. These students also have become publishers by posting material on blogs and participating in online discussions. This chapter addresses the extent to which these experiences are changing how students think about free expression in our society.

Finally, chapter 6 summarizes the data and findings, then offers a host of policy recommendations. The findings suggest a number of reforms that might positively influence the high school curriculum and the integration of new media technologies, ultimately improving student orientations toward free expression in America.

Data and Research Supporting the Book

A grant from the John S. and James L Knight Foundation produced two research studies of high school students from across the nation. These studies, conducted in 2004 and 2006 by two of the authors of this book (Kenneth Dautrich and David Yalof), are referred to as the Future of the First Amendment (FOFA) surveys. The Knight studies also featured surveys of principals and teachers. This book largely draws on the data collected in these studies to examine the role of the media and the high school curriculum in influencing student attitudes about the First Amendment. A number of research reports, special analyses of these data, and high school program materials have been developed as a result of these studies. For more information on these materials, see www.firstamendmentfuture.org.

In this book, we refer to the 2004 Knight Future of the First Amendment survey as "FOFA 2004" and to the 2006 survey as "FOFA 2006." We rely particularly heavily on the FOFA 2006, which profiled student uses of the so-called digital media. Therefore, appendix A provides an integrated copy of the survey instruments used in this project. The 2004 survey included interviews with over 114,000 students nationally, nearly 8,000 teachers, and over 300 principals from a random selection of 350 schools. In FOFA 2006, we drew a sample of 45 of the initial 350 schools and went back to interview 14,000 students and 800 teachers. These rich data sets provide large sample sizes from which to dig deep into select subgroups, which we do in this book and in the other reports and materials produced from the Knight funding. Appendix B provides a description of the research methods used to conduct FOFA 2004 and FOFA 2006. Appendix C features results of the full multivariate models used to test many of the relationships that lie at the heart of this book's argument.

In chapter 1 we also make frequent reference to a set of annual surveys of American adults, funded by the Freedom Forum's First Amendment Center. This annual survey, also directed by two of the authors of this book (Dautrich and Yalof), is referred to as the State of the First Amendment (SOFA). It has been conducted annually since 1997. These annual surveys include national samples of one thousand Americans. The First Amendment Center's website (www.fac.org) includes details on the methods and questions used in the State of the First Amendment projects, which we reference in this book as "SOFA."

Notes

1. E. E. Schattschneider, *The Semisovereign People: A Realist's View of Democracy in America* (New York: Holt, Rinehart and Winston, 1960).

2. Cited in Linda Monk, *The Words We Live By: Your Annotated Guide to the Constitution* (New York: Hyperion, 2003), 9.

3. Peter Levine, *The Future of Democracy: Developing the Next Generation of American Citizens* (Medford, MA: Tufts University Press), 2007.

4. See Lynne Lancaster and David Stillman, *When Generations Collide: Who They Are. Why They Clash. How to Solve the Generational Problem at Work* (New York: Collins, 2003); Neil Howe, William Strauss, and R. J. Matson, *Millennials Rising: The Next Generation* (New York: Vintage, 2000).

1

The American Public, Students, and Free Expression Rights

W HAT DO AMERICANS IN GENERAL, and high school students in particular, know and think about free expression rights? If the so-called digital media are changing the nature of publishing, and technology is influencing speech and press rights in the cyberworld, what are the baseline orientations regarding support for free expression? What do students know and think about freedom of the press and speech, and how does this compare with students' adult counterparts? Are students behind the curve, or do they exhibit similar (or even higher) levels of support for free expression than adults? Before we begin to explore how the digital media and educational system are shaping student opinion about free expression rights, it is first useful to understand where we are starting from; that is, what is the current status of speech and press freedoms from the perspective of high school students, and how do they compare to American adults?

The Dynamics of Support for Free Expression Rights

Liberty and free expression rights are hallmark characteristics of American democracy. The two go hand in hand. Public leaders, teachers, historians, and journalists all trumpet the values of free speech and free press as a core and defining element of American political culture.[1] But Americans' relationship with free expression rights is complex and often nuanced. While widely endorsed in principle, these freedoms are often quickly set aside, or at least assessed with caveats and conditions applied. Four sets of research findings characterize the dynamics of support for free expression.

High Support for Freedom of Expression at the Broad Level, Less in Specific Situations

It is a well-documented property of public opinion about individual liberties that, at the broad, abstract level, people exhibit high levels of support and affinity for "freedom," but when those freedoms are translated into concrete scenarios, the support often wanes to lower levels. Pioneering work in this area by Stouffer,[2] Prothro and Grigg,[3] and McCloskey[4] focused on the topic of political tolerance and generally concluded that Americans were quite supportive of the notion of freedom, liberty, and the general value of freedom of expression. However, when it came to specific situations in which Communist sympathizers, Nazis, or homosexuals might apply these freedoms, the willingness to afford such freedoms dropped considerably.

McCloskey and Brill further concluded that expression rights (compared to criminal due process rights, for example) are particularly subject to this dynamic. While these rights are "[so] widely endorsed by both the general public and opinion leaders as to suggest that freedom of expression may very well be the most cherished of American rights," they, at the same time, may be "the most tenuous right."[5] For example, while as many as 60 percent of Americans in the McCloskey and Brill study were willing to grant free speech rights generally to people whom they considered intolerant of others, only 18 percent would have permitted the American Nazi Party to use a public meeting hall.

More recent data tend to confirm these findings. For example, from a national survey conducted in 1999 (see table 1.1), Yalof and Dautrich[6] found that 81 percent of Americans say that freedom of speech is a right "essential" to American democracy, and 75 percent say that freedom of the press is similarly "essential." Other key findings include the fact that nearly three-quarters of Americans (72 percent) disagree that the First Amendment goes too far in the rights it guarantees. On press rights in particular, the public also expresses majority support: nearly six in ten do not feel that the press has too much freedom.

In addition, Yalof and Dautrich find that 90 percent of Americans agree with the statement "People should be allowed to express their opinion, whatever that opinion might be." Their research also shows that the vast majority of adults reject the general notion of censorship: 79 percent agree with the statement "Newspapers should be allowed to publish freely without government approval of a story."

The public widely supports contemporary opinions about free expression rights, as well as many other basic freedoms guaranteed by the Constitution—at least at this broad, abstract level. But when these broad, alluring principles of liberty and freedom are translated into specific situations, the public taste for allowing the exercise of expression rights often turns sour. For example,

Table 1.1
General Support for Various Freedoms and Liberties

"I am going to read you some rights guaranteed by the U.S. Constitution. For each, please tell me how important it is that you have that right—is it essential that you have this right, important but not essential, or not important that you have this right."

	% Saying Essential
The right to speak freely about what you want	81%
The right to assemble, march, protest, or petition the government	71%
The right to practice the religion of your choice	91%
The right to practice no religion	71%
The right to be informed by a free press	75%
The right to own firearms	33%
The right to privacy	85%
The right to a fair trial	95%

Source: Freedom Forum's 1999 SOFA survey.

should musicians be allowed to sing songs with lyrics that might be offensive? A bare majority (51 percent) think they should.[7] Should people be allowed to say things in public that might be offensive to racial groups? Only 41 percent say yes. Should people be allowed to display art with content that others might find offensive? Again, less than a majority (41 percent) think they should. Should people be allowed to publish sexually explicit material in magazines? Forty-five percent answer yes.[8]

Moreover, only 27 percent of adults think that public school students should be allowed to wear a T-shirt with a message or picture that others might find offensive. Further, the American public readily agrees with censorship of broadcast television: 67 percent say the government should be allowed to restrict sexually explicit material on TV; 60 percent say the government should be allowed to restrict violence on TV; and 57 percent say government restrictions on curse words used on TV are acceptable.

These findings suggest that people have a bifurcated view of free expression rights. At a broad, conceptual level, people are quite supportive of these liberties, as they are of other liberties engrained in the American political culture. But when situational contexts are considered, particularly ones in which affording the right to expression also endorses personally objectionable expression, support drops.

Public Support for Free Expression Rights Is Relative to Support for Other Values Engrained in American Political Culture

American political culture is defined by a wide array of values and principles beyond individual liberties and freedoms associated with free expression.

Individualism, diversity, limited government, equality of opportunity, security, and majority rule are among the many guiding tenets that underlie the American political psyche. Furthermore, while these values are in and of themselves heralded as important to the American political identity, at the same time they are often in conflict with each other.

Conflicts between these values are readily apparent. Individualism promotes and rewards the talents, energy, hard work, and intelligence of American citizens. Equality seeks to create a level playing field of fairness and opportunity for success. These values, however, often run head first into one another in a variety of situations. Take college admissions, for example. The value of individualism suggests that applicants to college should be judged and admitted on the basis of their accomplishments (SAT scores, high school grades, success in extracurricular activities, etc.). Yet, for some, the value of equality suggests that due to the troubling history of slavery and racism, certain ethnic minority groups (in particular, African Americans) are, by nature of their background, at an unfair disadvantage in college admissions.

The highly debated policy of affirmative action in college admissions is an example of a conflict that pits one value, individualism (admissions should be based on the past performance of the individual applicant), against another, equality (admissions should consider factors beyond the individual accomplishments of the applicant, such as race). The U.S. Supreme Court's divided opinion on the validity of using race as a factor in admissions at the University of Michigan[9] demonstrates just how difficult the conflicts can be to resolve.

Much like this value conflict, the value of liberty often finds itself in conflict with other core values. A shift in public opinion about press rights as a result of the September 11, 2001, terrorist attacks on the Pentagon and World Trade Center provides evidence of such a conflict between liberty and security. While Americans support free expression, they also desire to be secure, and they expect government to do what is necessary to provide for their safety. The terrorist attacks represented a direct threat to the safety and security of American citizens. About three thousand people lost their lives on September 11, and the public's concerns about its own security were placed into question.

With the heightened sense of vulnerability to terrorism, many saw free expression rights as conflicting with the government's ability to achieve greater security for the people. The annual State of the First Amendment surveys from 2000 through 2005 demonstrate how Americans' response to September 11 and that event's security threat altered the public's sense of freedom provided by the First Amendment.

In the month after the September 11 terrorist attacks in 2001, the percentage of Americans who said that the freedoms guaranteed by the First Amendment went too far nearly tripled, from 10 percent to 29 percent (see table 1.2). By the middle of 2002, the shock and concern brought on by details of how

Table 1.2
Support for Freedom Guaranteed by First
Amendment, Pre– and Post–September 11, 2001

"Based on your own feelings about the First Amendment, please tell me whether you strongly agree, mildly agree, mildly disagree, or strongly disagree with the following statement: "The First Amendment goes too far in the rights it guarantees.""

	% Who Strongly Agree
2000	10%
2001	29%
2002	41%
2003	19%
2004	19%
2005	13%

Source: These data are drawn from the Freedom Forum's SOFA surveys, 2000–2005.

the attacks were carried out, as well as discussion of whether further attacks might occur, in part led 41 percent of Americans to agree strongly that the First Amendment went too far in the rights it affords.

The desire for government to provide greater security and protection led many people to discount the importance of restricting government's ability to limit individual freedom. But as the years passed into 2003, 2004, and 2005, and the security threat subsided, Americans' feelings about First Amendment freedoms returned to their pre–September 11 levels, thus highlighting the ongoing tension between liberty and other firmly rooted values, as well as the dynamic nature of opinions about freedom.

Opinions about Liberty and Free Expression
Are Not Rooted in High Levels of Knowledge and Understanding

Whereas free expression rights are concepts that most Americans agree are an essential part of democracy, there does not appear to be a great deal of knowledge about the legal rules that govern these rights. For example, while about six in ten Americans are able to identify "freedom of speech" as a right guaranteed by the First Amendment, a paltry 16 percent can identify freedom of the press.[10]

The American public is similarly naïve when it comes to the specific meaning of free press and speech rights. For example, Yalof and Dautrich[11] found in 2002 that only 33 percent of Americans believe that people have the legal right to burn an American flag as a political statement, while 37 percent think that courts can send reporters to jail for refusing to divulge a news source.

Further, a majority (53 percent) wrongly believe that the government has the right to restrict indecent material on the Internet.

Americans are, however, self-critical of their lack of knowledge and understanding about free expression rights. Many believe not only that others in American society tend to take the First Amendment for granted but that they themselves are accustomed to doing so. Specifically, Yalof and Dautrich in a 1999 Freedom Forum survey found that fully 87 percent of Americans think that "other people" took the First Amendment for granted, and a majority (54 percent) admit that they personally took for granted the rights they were guaranteed.

The lack of knowledge, understanding, and appreciation of First Amendment rights may help to explain why support for free expression rights is so malleable, as was documented earlier in this chapter. Given a low level of knowledge regarding how these rights apply to contemporary society, it should not be too surprising that the high level of general support does not translate into high levels of support for free expression rights at the more concrete level. Further, the low level of knowledge also provides an explanation for why Americans might withdraw their affinity for free expression rights when other events, such as the terrorist threats to national security, confront the nation.

Public Perceptions of the Performance of the Press
Help Shape Attitudes about Freedom of the Press

Traditionally, free press rights were the province of the media, exercised primarily by book publishers, magazines and newspapers, and radio and television stations. Indeed, most Americans did not have the resources to make use of press rights effectively. That changed with the advent of the Internet, which allows any user the ability to distribute his or her views, and thus stake a claim to exercising the right to free press. The accessibility of the Internet affords anyone with a computer and Internet connection the ability to publish. Of course, many Americans, particularly older Americans, neither blog nor publish using the new technologies (see table 1.3). Therefore, for many Americans, press rights still pertain, from their perspective, to the media, and not to everyone. Even those who use the Internet to publish their ideas or thoughts may not think of "press rights" as available to them.

A common understanding of press rights, then, includes the guarantees and protections provided to the press and the media. In thinking about press rights, many are naturally drawn to consider how journalists, authors, talk radio hosts, news anchors, and other members of the professional press corps perform. As a result, Americans' attitudes about freedom of the press are in part a function of their opinions about the performance of the press.

Table 1.3
Use of Digital Media by American Public and High School Students in 2006

	Adults (18 and Over)	High Schoolers
Has access to the Internet	75%	87% at home 97% at school
Uses blogs	23%	48%
Gets news and information from Internet providers (e.g., Google, Yahoo!, MSN)	50%	88%
Participates in online discussions	17%	59%
Gets news and information from national newspaper websites	27%	47%
Gets news and information from local newspaper websites	43%	60%
Sends or receive e-mails	65%	85%

Source: Freedom Forum's 2006 SOFA survey and Knight's 2006 FOFA survey.

At best, Americans offer lukewarm assessments of the overall performance of the news media. A 2005 survey[12] found that 41 percent offer the news media a rating of either "excellent" (5 percent) or "good" (36 percent), while 40 percent say they are doing a "fair" job, and 18 percent give a rating of "poor."[13] As table 1.4 shows, the news media receive similarly lukewarm ratings in the job of educating people about complex issues, reporting information accurately, and holding public officials accountable. However, the media receive considerably higher evaluations for providing broad coverage of current events.

The mediocre ratings indicated in table 1.4 may be at least partially based on the perception of falsified news stories, which made headlines at the time

Table 1.4
Ratings of News Media Performance, 2006

	Excellent	Good	Fair	Poor	Don't Know
"Overall, how would you rate the job the news media are doing?"	5%	36%	40%	18%	0%
"How good a job do the news media do in educating the public about complex issues?"	5%	35%	37%	22%	1%
"How good a job do the news media do in reporting information accurately?"	4%	34%	42%	19%	1%
"How good a job do the news media do in keeping public officials accountable?"	6%	35%	39%	18%	1%
"How good a job do the news media do in providing broad coverage of current events?"	16%	46%	27%	11%	0%

Source: University of Connecticut survey of one thousand American adults conducted in May 2006.

these surveys were taken. One salient example was the story run by CBS news anchor Dan Rather regarding George W. Bush's National Guard records. Rather was forced to retract the story on the basis that it used falsified information, a story that we take up in greater detail in chapter 4. Still, the 2005 Freedom Forum State of the First Amendment survey found that fully 62 percent of Americans agree that "falsifying or making up stories in the American news media is a widespread problem." Further, when asked how often they trust journalists to tell the truth, only 6 percent say they trust journalists "all of the time," 72 percent trust them "some of the time," 15 percent trust them "a little of the time," and 7 percent do not trust them at all.

Comparing High School Students with the American Public on Free Expression Attitudes

As chapter 2 discusses, civic education has always been an important goal of the nation's schools. While the scope of the civics curriculum varies from state to state, district to district, and school to school, high schools across the nation take seriously their important mission to promote citizenship through social studies classes on democracy, voting, and the values underlying the American political system, which include the First Amendment's free expression rights. One might expect, then, that the high schools' orientation toward civics education might provide an environment for students to be more attentive to liberties and freedoms than they otherwise might be once they have completed school. One important goal of the Knight Foundation's Future of the First Amendment project was to assess whether the high school experience has somehow inspired a greater level of thought and reflection on First Amendment issues than people might normally give them later in life in an environment less structured for civics thinking.

To that end, the 2004 and 2006 Knight Foundation FOFA surveys of high school students repeat a number of questions asked on national general-public surveys to facilitate a comparison of American adults with American high school students. Here is what we find in comparing students to their adult counterparts:

1. *Students are more likely than adults to take their First Amendment rights for granted.* A Freedom Forum survey[14] found that less than a majority (42 percent) of adults said that they "personally think about" the rights they are guaranteed by the First Amendment. The Knight FOFA 2006 high school student survey found that a paltry 27 percent of students thought this way. It appears that high school students, despite being in

an environment where social studies and other classes promote the learning of democratic values such as freedom and liberty, are even less thoughtful about their First Amendment rights than are adults.

2. *Students are more apt to believe that the First Amendment goes too far in the rights that it guarantees.* Since 1999, the Freedom Forum SOFA survey has been asking whether or not people think the First Amendment goes overboard in the liberties that it guarantees. The item begins by presenting the actual text of the First Amendment to the respondent, then asking, "Based on your own feelings about the First Amendment, please tell me whether you agree or disagree with the following statement: the First Amendment goes too far in the rights it guarantees." In the SOFA 2005 survey, 72 percent of adults disagreed that the First Amendment goes too far, which may be interpreted as a healthy sign for public opinion about free expression rights. However, student responses to this question in the Knight FOFA 2006 survey reveal that the health of the First Amendment from the students' perspective is less certain. Specifically, the percentage of students who disagreed that the First Amendment goes too far is 37 percent, which is about half that of adults. Once again, it appears that American high school students are much more unappreciative of the First Amendment than adults.

3. *Students are more supportive of government censorship of newspapers than are adults, but they are less supportive of school-authority censorship of student newspapers than are adults.* When Americans were presented in the Freedom Forum's SOFA 2003 survey with the statement "Newspapers should be allowed to publish freely without government approval of a story," 70 percent said they agreed. When students in 2006 were presented with the exact same statement, a bare majority, 54 percent, agreed.

   Interestingly, however, student support for the right to publish freely in school newspapers exceeds that of adults. Specifically, in 2006, 64 percent of students agreed that "high school students should be allowed to report controversial issues in their student newspapers without the approval of school authorities," whereas only 43 percent of adults surveyed in 2004 agreed with that statement. Why might student rejection of school authority's censorship be greater than student rejection of governmental censorship? It may be that the perceived relevance of free expression rights has some bearing on support for such rights. When students are asked about government censorship of newspapers, students may have a harder time understanding how censorship might adversely affect them. However, when asked about school-authority censorship, perhaps an understanding of the value of free expression rights is clearer and more relevant. Students might be better able to understand why it is important that they or their fellow students be able to express themselves on a controversial issue at school than they can when the issue is more removed from their day-to-day experiences. This finding suggests that the more relevant rights are to individuals, the more likely they are to value such rights.

It is also notable that adults are more supportive of newspapers' rights to publish without government censorship (70 percent) than they are of student newspapers' rights to publish without the school authority's advance review (43 percent). Adults may be more likely to consider a value conflict with respect to the rights of students to publish without review. For adults, many of whom are or have been parents of high school–age kids, school safety tends to be a very high priority. The recent cases of school violence and school shootings heightens this public concern for student safety, which many may perceive as conflicting with the rights of students to express themselves on controversial issues at school. Adults may perceive such free expression as serving to inflame tensions at school or even incite unsafe situations. Certainly, principals and teachers view students' rights to express themselves without prior restraint of school authorities as more expendable, as table 1.5 demonstrates.

While the "occupational hazards" of free speech in a school newspaper undoubtedly influence low support for student press rights on the part of teachers and principals, this low support nonetheless must be examined. If teachers and principals are disinclined toward student press rights, what type of example does this offer to students as they develop their citizenship skills? If teachers and principals do not encourage (or, worse yet, discourage) students to actually use their free expression

Table 1.5
Support for High School Students'
Free Press Rights, 2004

"Do you agree or disagree with the following statement: high school students should be allowed to report controversial issues without approval of school authorities."

	Percent Agreeing
Students	58%
Adults	43%
Teachers	39%
Principals	13%

Source: SOFA 2004 and FOFA 2004.

rights by speaking out on important school issues in the school news-paper, then what is this teaching students about the value of press rights in our society? While student free expression may serve to promote con-troversy, debate, and even embarrassment, it also teaches that press rights are so important that they are worth promoting, despite the pos-sibly uncomfortable consequences they might produce.

4. *A strong majority of students believe that people should be allowed to ex-press unpopular opinions, but virtually all adults feel that way. However, when it comes to a form of speech that students particularly enjoy (music), student support for speech rights exceeds adult support.* A measure of dif-fuse support for free expression used regularly in the Freedom Forum's annual SOFA survey asks respondents whether they agree or disagree with this statement: "People should be allowed to express unpopular opinions." In the SOFA 2004 survey, fully 95 percent of American adults agreed with this general principal. The FOFA 2006 Knight survey of stu-dents found that a very strong majority (85 percent) agreed with this general orientation toward free expression. While 85 percent is very high, it still should be noted that students' diffuse level of support for free speech falls ten percentage points short of that of adults.

As described earlier in the chapter, most other research on the topic of diffuse and specific support generally finds that support at the broad, dif-fuse level is high but tends to wane when specific circumstances and/or particular people or groups are used to define speech in the form of un-popular opinions.[15] For example, while most support the general idea of allowing someone to say what's on their mind, support slips considerably when the speaker is identified as a "Nazi," "Communist," or "Islamic ex-tremist." Support tends to drop even further when such a disliked speaker speaks to a particularly vulnerable or offended audience, such as a Nazi speaking in a Jewish community or a homosexual teaching in a socially conservative public school. At the specific support level, the more offen-sive the speaker or group becomes and the more vulnerable the audience, the less likely respondents are to endorse the rights of free expression.

With the Knight FOFA student surveys, we included an item that at-tempts to reexamine this diffuse/specific support finding. The item asks respondents to agree or disagree with this statement: "Musicians should be allowed to sing songs with lyrics that others might find offensive." In-stead of specifying an offensive speaker, we specified a group that we thought students would positively identify with, namely, musicians. We wanted the item to suggest that the nature of the speech (i.e., song lyrics), however, could still be regarded as offensive. Certainly, most young peo-ple are familiar with music, and most might readily understand that some lyrics in some songs they have heard might be offensive to certain people. This measure of specific support is intended to examine students' responses to a specific speech situation that they might readily identify with and regard as important, while at the same time suggesting that some parts of the audience might be offended by the speech. Essentially, we believe the item redefines the specific situation to make the free expression more personally relevant to the student-respondents, rather than more distant (e.g., a Communist). We also included this item on the adult surveys for the Freedom Forum, enabling us to compare and contrast how adults and students respond. Table 1.6 depicts the findings on this item for students and adults and juxtaposes the findings of this specific support measure with the general support measure for free expression rights.

The table shows that among students, nearly seven in ten agree that musicians should be allowed to sings songs with lyrics that might be offensive to some people. This is ten points higher than the number of adults who are willing to afford musicians such speech rights. While adults are more likely to support the more generalized measure of speech rights, students are in fact more supportive of free expression in this specific situation. The implications of this finding are significant. When the abstract notion of free expression rights is translated to a situation where respondents are able to identify with those who are afforded the rights, support for the rights remains high. While there is some drop-off in support for the more generalized measure (85 percent to 69 percent), a substantial majority still supports the rights. The relevance of the situation to the students (again, assuming that music and song lyrics are particularly important forms of speech to high school–age students) heightens their support for free expression. This finding also suggests that the way in which high school classes go about teaching the First Amendment can be important as well. If the content of these classes includes situations that energize student learning, such as a discussion of how music and song lyrics are a form of speech, students will better relate to and learn about the value of free expression rights.

Table 1.6
General Support and Specific Support for Free Expression Rights

	Adults, 2005	Students, 2006
Percentage agreeing that people should be allowed to express unpopular opinions	95%	85%
Percentage agreeing that musician should be allowed to sing songs with offensive lyrics	59%	69%

Source: SOFA 2005 and FOFA 2006.

5. *Students are less knowledgeable about how speech rights may or may not be used than are adults.* As noted earlier in this chapter, many adults do not correctly understand the types of expression that the First Amendment does and does not protect. But student knowledge is even lower than that of adults. The student survey shows, for example, that only 25 percent of high school students believe that Americans have the legal right to burn the flag as an expression of political protest, compared to 33 percent of adults. In addition, only 31 percent of students think that the courts can jail reporters for refusing to reveal a news source (37 percent of adults think this), and 49 percent of students believe that government has the right to restrict indecent material on the Internet (compared to 40 percent of adults).

Changes in Students Attitudes: 2004 to 2006

While the data on student support for free expression rights suggest that the future of the First Amendment may be in peril, there are some signs that student opinion may be on the rise. A comparison of the 2004 and 2006 FOFA student surveys, which repeated the same questions, facilitates the tracking of changes over this period.

In 2006, for example, 41 percent of students said that the press in America has "about the right amount of freedom," which is a four-percentage-point improvement since 2004. Also, in 2006, the 64 percent of students who agree that high school students should be allowed to report controversial issues in their student newspapers without the approval of school authorities represents a six-percentage-point increase over the two-year period. A smaller three-point increase occurred among those who agree that newspapers should be allowed to publish freely without government approval of a story. In 2006, 85 percent of students agreed that people should be allowed to express unpopular opinions, which represents a small two-point improvement (statistically significant due to the large sample sizes) since 2004.

What might account for these small, but positive, changes? As chapter 2 documents, there was a reported increase in the percentage of students who had taken classes with First Amendment, media, and journalism skills content. These increases may have been spurred by several events over the 2004–2006 period, including any and all of the following: (1) the national discussion in the press and elsewhere over the federal government's alleged intrusion on liberties and freedoms as part of its declared "war on terrorism"; (2) the passage of legislation in 2004 creating a national Constitution Day, which mandates that all schools receiving federal funding designate a day to focus on important constitutional issues, including the First Amendment; and (3) the increased attention given by national advocacy groups, such as the Journalism Education Association, the Columbia Scholastic Press Association, the American Society of Newspaper Editors, and others, to First Amendment topics in general and to student views of the First Amendment in particular. These factors may in part account for these modest, but significant, improvements in student orientations toward free expression rights.

Conclusion

In many ways, the findings from the Knight FOFA high school student surveys amount to a "call to arms." The future health of the First Amendment seems questionable, given students' low levels of support and appreciation for free expression rights. Free speech and free press rights are bedrocks of American democracy. These rights guarantee a free marketplace of ideas, energy in national policy debates, an informed public, and a government that will be held accountable to the people. Free expression also promotes society's collective search for truth. It promotes the expression of opinions and ideas that are "outside the box." It encourages scientific discovery and advancement. It serves as a check on the power of authority and promotes the value of limited government. Moreover, free expression serves to promote the American commitment to individual liberty and personal autonomy. How safe and secure are these principles if the next generation of Americans is not grounded in proper levels of support for free expression rights?

In the remainder of this book, we examine two factors, or "agents of socialization," that may positively influence high school students' formation and development of more positive orientations toward the First Amendment. These factors include the curriculum and extracurricular activities in America's high schools and the special relationship that today's students have with the so-called digital media. In chapters 2 through 5 of the book, we examine how America's high schools and the changing nature of communication through the "new media" may be altering students' orientation toward free expression and discuss how these factors may be used to further promote positive change.

Notes

1. See Richard Merelman, *Making Something of Ourselves: On Culture and Politics in the United States* (Berkeley: University of California Press, 1984).

2. Samuel Stouffer, *Communism, Conformity and Civil Liberties* (New York: Doubleday, 1955).

3. J. Prothro and C. Grigg, "Fundamental Principles of Democracy: Bases of Agreement and Disagreement," *Journal of Politics* 22 (1960): 276–94.

4. Herbert McCloskey and Alida Brill, *Dimensions of Tolerance: What Americans Believe about Civil Liberties* (New York: Russell Sage Foundation, 1983).

5. McCloskey and Brill, *Dimensions of Tolerance*, 48.

6. David Yalof and Kenneth Dautrich, *The First Amendment and the Media in the Court of Public Opinion* (New York: Cambridge University Press, 2002).

7. From the Freedom Forum SOFA-2005 survey.

8. From the Freedom Forum SOFA-2005 survey.

9. See *Grutter v. Bollinger*, 539 U.S. 306 (2003); *Gratz v. Bollinger*, 529 U.S. 244 (2003).

10. Yalof and Dautrich, *The First Amendment and the Media*, 2002.

11. Yalof and Dautrich, *The First Amendment and the Media*, 2002.

12. SOFA 2005.

13. Other data sources also suggest that Americans have a lukewarm assessment of the press. According to Monitoring the Future, in 1976 63 percent of high school seniors said they approved of the job the media was doing. In 2005, only 41 percent said the same. According to the American National Election Study, in 1996 36 percent of adults said they trusted the media "just about always" or "most of the time"; by 2004, that figure had fallen slightly to 35 percent. Tabulations for both data sources are available upon request.

14. Data drawn from the 1999 Freedom Forum SOFA survey.

15. See Stouffer, *Communism, Conformity and Civil Liberties*; Prothro and Grigg, "Fundamental Principles of Democracy"; McCloskey and Brill, *Dimensions of Tolerance*.

2

Educating Students about
Free Expression Rights

"Civic education," or "civics," generally refers to education in the rights and obligations of citizens, as well as the laws that govern them. To be sure, some form of civics has found its way into the curriculum of schools since the beginning of the Republic. This was not by accident. The American Constitution, ratified in 1788 and put into practice in 1789, was "strictly republican" in the sense that the new government was expected to derive all its powers directly or indirectly from the people, who would then express their will both through majority vote and public opinion. The new American government relied largely on fostering within the polity "civic virtues," the cultivation of habits of personal living deemed important to the community's success. Among the civic virtues considered most essential to the survival of the early Republic was "an appreciative understanding of how the system works" that necessarily extends beyond a "passive or merely occasional interest in federal and state politics."[1]

Civic education wasn't just one of many important issues to be addressed by this young nation; for those in the founding generation, it was the first order of business. Prior to the revolution, John Adams wrote that "wherever a general knowledge and sensibility have prevailed among the people, arbitrary government and every kind of oppression have lessened and disappeared in proportion."[2] How and in what fashion does such knowledge get transmitted? In his first annual message to Congress, George Washington argued that the national government needed to support an education for citizens that would teach them "to know and to value their own rights; to discern and provide against invasions of them."[3] In a public statement on schooling he penned while contemplating the creation of the University of Virginia, Thomas Jefferson stated publicly that the goal of education was to give to every citizen "the information he needs for the transaction of his own business," including "to know his rights; to exercise with order and justice those he retains."[4]

More recently, Jaroslav Pelikan has argued that "connecting public education to citizenship" requires first that there be widespread access of the youngest of citizens to schools where civic education occurs.[5] Expressions of support for civic education such as those by America's founders had occurred even before a formal public school system was put into place. Today, state-supported schools serve as the central institutions for teaching citizens civic skills, but that was not the case before the latter half of the nineteenth century. In the 1850s and 1860s, a few states began to experiment with an "oddly American notion of education" financed by the public. It took half a century before individual states established local school districts and free common schools became the emerging norm.[6] Even then, the "single red schoolhouse in the town center" remained the standard for three out of four families throughout America.

Secondary education for those beyond the age of fourteen was reserved primarily for elites; as late as 1900, it was still common for public high schools to maintain entrance examinations that limited high school admission to fewer than 5 percent of the population. The remaining 95 percent were expected to take a job and care for their families instead of going to high school. It wasn't until the middle part of the twentieth century that comprehensive high schools offering a free education for twelve years to get a diploma began to take hold universally. With a mandatory attendance age of sixteen in most states, school districts were for the first time challenged to minimize the number of students who exited at sixteen.

Teaching the students the three R's was certainly one means of preparing students to become participants in a democracy. Even the Amish, who challenged compulsory education in the junior high school and high school years, deferred to the requirement that children accept that form of mandatory education.[7] What seemed less compelling to some ethnic and religious minorities was the state's interest in socializing children to America's political values. And yet, that socialization requirement has always been central to the purposes of public and private education.

Civics and Political Socialization

The founders were committed to civic education for America's youth because they understood that patterns and orientations adopted early on embed themselves in a person's overall political and civic outlook. Theories of political so-cialization, "the developmental processes through which persons acquire polit-ical orientations and patterns of behavior,"[8] are based on this simple premise: what people learn prior to adulthood significantly affects their political life.

David Easton in particular did groundbreaking research on this subject. Specifically, he examined how political systems remain stable despite a con-tinually changing world. Easton found that "diffuse" support (i.e., deeply held positive feelings toward the political system) effectively provide a cushion for the system from debilitating external shocks.[9] Why do students express such diffuse support? According to Easton, it is a product of the socialization that occurs within them long before they are adults.

Today, it has become widely accepted among scholars that schools, aided by families and peer groups, serve as primary agents of political socialization. Schools make a unique contribution in this regard. Certainly, government can pass laws that direct (or strongly encourage) citizens to engage in political ac-tivities. Compulsory voting laws, for example, can be found in democracies such as Australia. Yet, whenever those laws change, so does the likelihood that citizens will continue their engagement. By comparison, schools can directly influence students' minds and outlooks and thus infuse values directly into their views on society, government, and laws. The importance of this direct in-fluence cannot be overstated.

When are students most susceptible to this influence? Apparently, children undergo a political "growth spurt" during adolescence.[10] Ironically, the orien-tation that shows the least amount of growth later in life is support for dem-ocratic values such as free speech and minority rights.[11] The two scholars who did groundbreaking research on this phenomenon were Herbert McCloskey and Alida Brill. In their seminal work, *Dimensions of Tolerance: What Ameri-cans Believe about Civil Liberties,*[12] they argue that considerable socialization is necessary to "appreciate the relation between First Amendment Freedoms and the issues with which these liberties must come to grips."[13] McCloskey and Brill confirm the "when" about such political socialization; they leave the more difficult question of "how" to others.

Much of the formal experimental work on the political socialization and civic development of adolescents has focused on how political events or civics cur-ricula impact political development. Negative political events like Vietnam, Wa-tergate, and the Clinton-Lewinsky scandal erode adolescents' mainly positive feelings about individuals who run the government. These negative events do not, however, impact students' support, knowledge, and appreciation of the po-litical system. David Sears and Nicholas Valentino have argued that children aged ten to seventeen learn about politics by observing common political events such as elections.[14] With a presidential campaign as a background, they found that adolescents did make "substantial gains" in attitude development regarding political parties and candidates over the course of the campaign period.[15]

What type of socialization effects does civic education instill? In 1975, M. Kent Jennings and Richard Niemi provided a framework of four types of socialization effects that may be at work: continuity over time, generational effects, life cycle effects, and period effects.[16] *Continuity over time* models obviously show little or no differences at all. By contrast, *life cycle effects* are changes endemic to the life course by which children and teenagers, as they pass through time, are brought into line with the older generation. *Generational differences* derive from age cohorts undergoing shared experiences and can lead to distinctive generational units of like-minded people. Finally, *period effects* reflect important events and trends of the time, with a roughly common effect produced on all or most segments.

High school students in particular are impressionable politically as they are at a stage in their life cycles when they are more prone to begin to think about politics and to develop a lasting set of values and orientations. Thus, a combination of life cycle effects and period effects appears to be at work among high school students. In this book, we investigate the degree to which new and old media experiences in particular influence high school students and affect their political values.

Unfortunately, research on the impact of social studies curricula on civic development to date has provided little in the way of a unifying theory to explain how this socialization occurs in the classroom. Part of the problem lies in the authoritarian social structure of many high schools, which runs counter to the principles required for good citizenship.[17] It is also exceedingly difficult to pinpoint the moment of socialization when a subject has been taught to students for years: some scholars contend that the high school civics curriculum simply reinforces the same democratic principles that students have been exposed to since primary school.[18]

Civic education about civil rights and liberties presents researchers with a different set of challenges, largely because comparatively fewer schools teach students about their liberties. Certainly, the positive relationship between support for civil liberties on one hand and years of formal schooling on the other hand is by now well established.[19] Even more significantly, students exposed to classroom education on civil liberties appear to shape their outlooks on liberties accordingly. In the late 1970s, Dennis Goldenson found in an experimental testing of high school students in Minnesota that students exposed to the civil liberties unit in social studies were three times more likely (27 percent to 8 percent) than students in a control group to show an increase in support for civil liberties.[20] Patricia Avery and her colleagues similarly used an experimental design to conclude that a social studies curriculum with a "systematic examination of the role of dissent in a democratic society" produces students with high levels of tolerance toward "disliked political groups."[21]

The scholarship to date has not really addressed more specifically whether classes or curricula that focus on the First Amendment as a whole and all the free expression rights encompassed within it, including press freedom, may potentially affect students' attitudes and tolerance toward those same freedoms. Although some connection may be assumed given these previous studies, the John S. and James L. Knight Foundation's Future of the First Amendment studies in 2004 and 2006 attempted to assess that connection in the context of high schools in the twenty-first century.

The First Amendment in the Nation's Public Schools

Do minors enjoy similar First Amendment rights as adults? Certainly, not all adult constitutional rights are equally applicable to students. Fourth Amendment rights, for example, are more limited in public schools. In *New Jersey v. T.L.O.* (1985),[22] the Supreme Court allowed school officials to conduct a warrantless search of students (specifically, one student's purse) because there was reason to suspect the search would turn up evidence of a violation of school rules or the law. Lower federal courts have similarly upheld searches of student lockers under the *T.L.O.* standard, and in 1985, the Supreme Court upheld the school-based drug testing of student athletes.[23] Although adults benefit from many due process rights, students do not, for example, have a right to the assistance of counsel, to question witnesses against them, or to call witnesses when they suffer short-term (i.e., ten days or less) suspensions from school. Students at every level of education enjoy extremely little due process protection when it comes to academic decisions such as grades.[24] In fact, in 1977 the Supreme Court upheld the use of corporal punishment against students without providing due process rights first.[25]

Still, from the outset, the Supreme Court has treaded far more cautiously in cases involving students' free expression rights, recognizing that there must be constitutional limits to the state's role in socializing children in public schools. As early as 1943, the Supreme Court held that students may not be compelled to salute the flag if it violates their personal beliefs.[26] At the same time, the Court has acknowledged that public schools have an interest in educating students about their responsibilities as citizens. Thus, school officials must effectively strike a balance between encouraging civic education in the public schools on one hand and allowing students to think and speak freely on the other.

In *Tinker v. Des Moines* (1967),[27] the Supreme Court was asked to resolve tensions between free speech and order in schools in the midst of a national debate over America's involvement in the Vietnam War. In order to protest that ongoing conflict, several students attending Des Moines High School and Des Moines Junior High School in December 1965 wore black armbands to class. In accordance with a school policy that banned the wearing of such armbands, three students were immediately sent home and suspended. By a 7–2 vote, the Supreme Court upheld the students' right to wear the armbands under the First Amendment. Critical to the Court's analysis was the absence of any lower court finding that students who wore black armbands had "materially disrupted" or intruded upon the work of the school.[28] Just as significantly, the Supreme Court in *Tinker* dismissed any notion that the First Amendment could only be exercised by adults in the United States. In an oft-quoted passage from the case, Justice Abe Fortas wrote that while school officials necessarily enjoy comprehensive authority to set and enforce school rules, neither students nor teachers "shed their constitutional rights to freedom of speech or expression at the schoolhouse gate."[29]

Although *Tinker* was clearly a victory for students' free expression rights, the "material disruption" doctrine has proven a mixed blessing in practice. According to the Supreme Court, whenever a material disruption to public education is discovered, speech in public schools may be highly controlled, if not outright prohibited. The limitations of the *Tinker* doctrine were on display in the case of *Bethel School District No. 403 v. Fraser* (1986).[30] In *Bethel*, a high school student gave a lewd speech at a school assembly of approximately six hundred students. Called forth to nominate a fellow student for elective office, Matthew Fraser delivered a speech laced with sexual innuendo, although no outright obscenity.[31] During the speech, some students hooted and made obscene gestures; others simply expressed embarrassment. When the school disciplined Fraser by suspending him for two days, he challenged his suspension in court. This time the Supreme Court, again by 7–2 vote, ruled that the school district had acted legitimately by imposing sanctions on Fraser in response to his "offensively lewd and indecent speech." Writing for the majority, Chief Justice Warren Burger wrote, "The First Amendment does not prevent school officials from determining that to permit a vulgar and lewd speech such as [his] would undermine the school's basic educational mission."

Where does that leave school officials in supervising student publications? Certainly, they enjoyed an improved position after *Bethel*, but how much better a position remained to be seen. The Supreme Court's only venture to date into the First Amendment implications of high school newspapers within the school building itself occurred two decades ago in *Hazelwood School District v. Kuhlmeier* (1988).[32] Unfortunately for those seeking clarity in the discussion, *Hazelwood* also left open as many questions as it answered and provided a truly complex maze for school officials to navigate in the years that followed.

Hazelwood considered the case of a student newspaper, the *Spectrum*, published by the Journalism II class at Hazelwood East High School in St. Louis, Missouri. The *Spectrum* had planned to publish two controversial stories: one involving three students' experience with pregnancy and another that discussed the impact of divorce on several students at the school. When the principal reviewed the page proofs and deleted the two stories from the newspaper, the students brought suit claiming that school officials had violated their First Amendment rights. The Supreme Court, by a 5–3 vote, denied the students' rights to publish the two stories over the principal's objections. Writing for the Court majority, Justice Byron White offered that the rights of students are not necessarily the same as those of adults in other settings: the *Spectrum* was not a forum for public expression by students; thus, the censored students could not count on the First Amendment for protection.

Hazelwood could have struck a devastating blow against scholastic journalism if it were open to broad interpretation. In fact, the ruling did not afford principals and school officials the equivalent of a free reign to determine what can and cannot be published. In particular, by ruling that the *Spectrum* was not a public forum, the Supreme Court in *Hazelwood* left open the possibility that some school-sponsored publications may be treated as public forums where First Amendment rights are fully applicable. In the case of the *Spectrum*, it was assumed that the journalism teacher or advisor would be the final authority on all content.[33] Moreover, the Hazelwood school district never explicitly labeled the student newspaper as a "forum" in its written policies; nor did it give any other evidence to make it a forum. Finally, as a creation of the school itself, the newspaper's very existence arose from decisions made by school officials. All this counseled in favor of a narrow application of the First Amendment.

Thus, *Hazelwood* implies that if a student publication is not school sponsored or part of the school curriculum, and if the publication has been treated as a public forum, it stands a good chance of falling under the more deferential *Tinker* standard. According to the Student Press Law Center, a group that advocates broad free press rights for students, "underground, alternative and even extracurricular publications" may retain much stronger First Amendment protections than a student newspaper published within the confines of a formal journalism class.[34] Examples of such underground publications abound. The Student Press Law Center reports that at an Arkansas high school in 1994, student journalists published and distributed a four-page newspaper outside of school after their principal ordered the paper's staff to submit to prior review a story about a student's fatal shooting; a group of New Jersey high school students similarly went underground in 1995 after their advisor left and the school refused to let them operate without one.[35] And in fact, federal courts have indicated that the history and method of operations utilized by a student newspaper might constitute significant factors in determining whether the publication amounted to a public forum for First Amendment purposes.[36]

Of course, *Hazelwood* was handed down almost two decades ago, before the advent of the Internet. At that time, the Supreme Court did not yet have the foresight to consider the possible issues that arise in the context of online expression. Unfortunately, the Supreme Court's most recent student expression case, *Morse v. Frederick* (2007),[37] only hinted at those issues without directly addressing them.

In *Morse*, the Supreme Court narrowly ruled against a student who had unfurled a banner reading "Bong Hits 4 Jesus" across the street from his high school in Juneau, Alaska. Many free speech advocates decried the high court's willingness to cut back on *Tinker* even further by allowing school officials to restrict any speech that is considered "vulgar and lewd."[38] And yet, once again, the Supreme Court left several critical student expression issues unanswered, including the thorny question of what constitutes "on-campus" expression and what may be considered "off-campus" expression. Student Joseph Frederick had argued that he should receive the full panoply of First Amendment protections that adults receive because he was not on school property when he displayed his banner, he had not even attended school that day, and he was eighteen years old. Some amicus briefs, including that of the Rutherford Institute, even urged the Court to examine the case as a non-school-speech case. The Supreme Court rejected that argument, although Chief Justice John Roberts acknowledged in the Court's opinion that "there is some uncertainty at the outer boundaries as to when courts should apply school-speech precedents." Online expression clearly offers the next great issue that the Court will wrestle with in this context.

Alternative Forms of Education: Extracurricular Activities and Students' Political Development

The influence and impact of classroom civics education on democracy is clear. Even the nation's courts have recognized a constitutional component to some aspects of student expression. By comparison, the positive effect of extracurricular activities that complement such high school curricula requires a bit more analysis and justification. Educators' interest in the importance of extracurricular activities to the overall development of children and adolescents only arose for the first time in the initial decades of the twentieth century. Unfortunately, school officials who encouraged such activities often ran into a competing perspective that such activities actually work against students attempting to focus on academic instruction. Many academic administrators feared that the increased popularity of extracurricular activities might serve to undermine overall student success in fulfilling the so-called main mission of schooling: academic instruction in reading, writing, and arithmetic within the classroom context.

In recent decades, all of those fears have been allayed both within and outside educational circles. Today, the overwhelming weight of scholarship suggests that extracurricular activities do have a positive influence on the educational development of students. Most of this research has tended to focus on the behavioral differences between participators and nonparticipators. Studies of these activities' specific benefits tend to fall into four different but related categories:

1. **The impact of extracurricular activities on academic achievement:** Involvement in a variety of extracurricular endeavors (church and volunteer activities, team sports, performing arts, academic clubs, etc.) has been linked to positive educational trajectories in general.[39] In one study, participation in such activities was directly linked to seventeen important senior and postsecondary outcomes, including educational aspirations, course work selection, better homework, decreased absenteeism, higher test scores, and subsequent college attendance.[40] More recent studies have focused on the impact of such activities on socioeconomically disadvantaged students in particular. Herbert Marsh and Sabina Kleitman, for example, found such activities play a role in fostering academic commitment by disadvantaged students, many of whom are least well served by aspects of the more traditional educational curriculum.

2. **The impact of extracurricular activities on student delinquency:** Scholars who have systematically studied the records of high school students across the country have generally reached the same conclusion: students who become heavily involved in extracurricular activities tend to be "model students" and only seldom are involved in delinquency and crime. This has been especially true of so-called high-risk children for whom declines in antisocial patterns depend heavily on social-network participation in extracurricular activities.[41]

3. **The impact of extracurricular activities on high school dropout rates:** Scholars have frequently conducted studies to assess the factors that influence high school dropout rates. Linkages between dropout rates and participation in extracurricular activities often depend on the nature of the activities themselves, as well as on breaking out the subgroups of students for more specific analysis. For example, in 1997 social scientists Joseph Mahoney and Robert Cairns found that school dropout rates

were lower for at-risk students who had participated in extracurricular activities, but the connection between the two was more modest when considering only those students judged "competent" or "highly competent" during middle school.[42] Another scholar discovered that while participation in athletics and fine arts significantly reduced a student's likelihood of dropping out, participation in academic or vocational clubs tended to have little or no effect.[43]

4. **The impact of extracurricular activities on civic engagement more generally:** Recently, several scholars have explored the links between participation in extracurricular activities and civic engagement. Generally, the consensus is that extracurricular activities can impart civic skills that may impact civic engagement later in life, such as the development of networks, leadership skills, and skills useful for collective action.[44]

Student Media Offerings: Influence and Impact

Student media and journalism programs across the country vary widely. Some journalism programs are embedded within the curriculum itself as an elective associated with the English program or some other formal academic class. Other student journalism programs consist entirely of student newspapers for which all student participation is optional. Many such programs in the latter category would be classified as a "prosocial activity" under the typology suggested by Eccles and Barber (1999). Applying the findings of these more general studies to student journalism programs, we may expect student participants to suffer from less risky behavior, demonstrate better academic performance, and exhibit a greater likelihood of being enrolled full-time in college after graduation. Student participation in high school newspapers in particular may also contribute to the cultivation of political literacy in general, as those students are more likely to take an interest in politics and participate in civic activities.[45]

Regardless of how the student media program is structured at any given high school, much of the scholarly research that has examined the impact of journalism programs has tended to focus exclusively on academic measures. Most notably, Jack Dvorak of Indiana University examined the performance of high school students on Advanced Placement (AP) English-language and -composition exams between 1989 and 1997. Dvorak found that "journalism kids do better": students who had taken an "intensive journalistic writing course" prior to taking the AP examination passed at a higher rate than those students who prepared for the exam by taking other advanced high school English courses.[46] John Robert Blinn systematically compared the work of journalism students to nonjournalism students in AP or honors composition classes in twelve Ohio schools; that study found that journalism students tended to make far fewer errors.[47] Dorothy McPhillips discovered that college students who had studied journalism or worked on school publications in high school performed better during their freshmen year of college than most other students.[48]

Some research has also examined levels of censorship in secondary school press operations. The impact of involvement with journalism activities or instruction on college students' academic success has also been intensively studied. Yet, no study to date has focused exclusively on participating high school students' knowledge of and attitudes toward free expression rights. Nor have the attitudes of teachers (and principals) toward the First Amendment ever been explored in this context. Interestingly, at least one survey directly assessed educators' opinions of *Hazelwood v. Kuhlmeier*; specifically, it closely examined teachers at schools featuring the power to censor some student-sponsored publications. Ten years after the ruling, 38 percent of journalism educators indicated that they thought *Hazelwood* was a good ruling, which was considerably less than the 71 percent of nonjournalism educators who felt that way and remarkably less than the 59 percent of the general public who favored the ruling. Yet, just 15 percent felt the ruling had provided less freedom to students, and no effort was made to go beyond the *Hazelwood* decision to assess attitudes toward press freedoms and the First Amendment more generally.

To further our understanding of the way that student media programs contribute not just to academic achievement in general but to political socialization of values held in particular, it will be necessary to address those items as well from the perspective of students, faculty, and administrators.

First Amendment Education in the Twenty-first Century:
A Profile of the Nation's High Schools

Unfortunately for interested students, most of the nation's high schools are not currently engaged in the process of finding new and innovative ways to expand their respective curricula to include units on the First Amendment; nor are most schools in the process of rapidly expanding their extracurricular student media offerings. At the turn of the twenty-first century, school budgets, already stretched to their limits, are, if anything, being squeezed further. School officials must grapple with demands that they educate more students at a cheaper price. Rather than focusing their energies on civics education, many of these officials have been forced to focus on reading, writing, and mathematics, because those are the subjects targeted by federal No Child Left Behind legislation.

The Knight Future of the First Amendment (FOFA) surveys in 2004 and 2006 provide an opportunity to profile the activities of high schools across the country, with special attention paid to the journalism curriculum, First Amendment instruction, and other media-related student activities.

Unfortunately, student journalism has yet to become a staple of most high school curricula. Fewer than one in ten (9 percent) of administrators at the 544 schools initially profiled in 2004 indicated that 20 percent or more of their students were currently enrolled in classes primarily dedicated to teaching journalism skills (see figure 2.1). And 16 percent of the administrators indicated that none of the students in their schools were currently enrolled in such classes (see figure 2.2).

Of those schools that did offer some type of student media activity, by far the most commonly offered type was the student-run newspaper. In fact, nearly three quarters (74 percent) of all the high schools in the United States indicated that they currently offered a student newspaper. By contrast, other types of media activities were offered by significantly fewer schools; less than a quarter offered any of the other activities.

Meanwhile, of the schools that did not currently offer a student newspaper at their school, a substantial percentage (40 percent) said they had eliminated their student papers within the past five years (see table 2.1). Among the 40 percent of schools that had dropped their student newspapers between 1999 and 2004, the majority (68 percent) now offered no student media activities. The remaining third of those schools that had eliminated student newspapers over that period still offered at least one student media activity, and several of these schools had added different types of media activities since 1998:

- 19 percent had Internet media (13 percent added since 1998)
- 3 percent had radio stations (2 percent added since 1998)
- 5 percent had magazines (2 percent added since 1998)

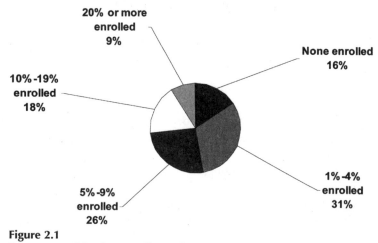

Figure 2.1
Percentage of Student Enrollment in Journalism Courses, 2004

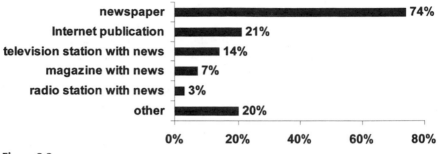

Figure 2.2
Student-run Journalism Activities/Clubs Offered in High Schools, 2004

A comparatively larger drop in the presence of school newspapers was found in lower-income schools between 1999 and 2004; a 16 percent decrease was found among upper-income schools, as compared to a 28 percent decrease among middle-income schools and a 37 percent decrease among lower- and middle-income schools. Although a 19 percent decrease in the presence of school newspapers occurred among the most socioeconomically disadvantaged schools, many within this latter category represented schools that most likely did not have a student newspaper. Additionally, table 2.1 shows the drop in the number of school newspapers was less pronounced in suburban schools than in urban or rural schools.

Table 2.1
Student Newspapers Dropped between 1999
and 2004 by Geographic Setting of School

School Type	Overall Percentage of Schools	Percentage That Dropped Student Newspaper in Past Five Years
Urban	19%	30%
Suburban	34%	16%
Rural	48%	54%

Source: FOFA 2004.

Curricular Offerings for Students

Students in 2004 and 2006 were asked a series of questions concerning the specific types of courses they took that addressed aspects of the First Amendment or the media. Some progress was evident in the two years that passed between the surveys; still, from the perspective of many First Amendment educators, there remains substantial room for reform.

While many students have taken general courses dealing with those subjects, significantly fewer have taken courses that deal specifically with learning journalism skills. Nevertheless the numbers here are on the upswing. In 2004, the majority (58 percent) of students surveyed indicated that had taken classes in high school that dealt with the First Amendment. In particular, a slightly higher percentage of public school students (59 percent) than private school students (54 percent) had taken classes that dealt with the First Amendment. Students in rural areas (61 percent) were also slightly more likely to have taken these types of classes than students in suburban (58 percent) and urban (56 percent) areas. Meanwhile, in 2006, fully 72 percent of students said they had taken at least one course that dealt with the First Amendment, a significant increase by any measure.

While the vast majority of students have had some experience in the classroom with using the media for specific class assignments, fewer have taken classes that specifically discuss the media's role in our society. In 2004, more than three-quarters (76 percent) of students said they had taken a course in which the teacher required them to read a newspaper or watch television news as a class assignment. By 2006, those numbers had increased to 81 percent. Yet, when it comes to courses that study the role of the media and how it impacts our society in various ways, fewer still (52 percent in 2004 and 62 percent in 2006) had taken such courses. Of course, as a more specialized type of course, the latter would probably fall into an elective category at most high schools.

What about classes that teach journalism skills? Overall, significantly fewer students have taken such courses. In 2004, less than a quarter (21 percent) of students said they had taken classes in high school that dealt primarily with journalism skills. A greater percentage of students from economically disadvantaged areas (26 percent) had taken such courses than students from higher-income areas: lower-middle income (22 percent), middle income (19 percent), and upper income (21 percent). The overall numbers went up slightly to 26 percent in 2006.

Student Media Activities

In 2004, over a quarter (27 percent) of the high school students surveyed said they did not spend any time during an average week participating in extracurricular activities. Of course, that means the great majority of students did spend some time participating in various extracurricular activities. Moreover, a full majority (56 percent) of students said they spent between one and fifteen hours engaging in such activities during an average week.

Certainly, students participate in a wide variety of clubs and activities ranging from sports, to performance arts, to school newspapers. However, when it comes to extracurricular activities, sports are the clear favorite among high school students; a majority (57 percent) of all students participate in sports clubs and teams. Many students (38 percent) also participate in performance arts, student government (15 percent), or debate/speech (11 percent) activities.

By contrast, when it comes to media-related extracurricular activities, a relatively low percentage of students in 2004 (less than 10 percent) indicated that they participated. Higher percentages (ranging from 17 to 32 percent, depending on the activity) said they would like to participate if the activity eventually became available at their school. Across the board, African American students were more likely than white students to participate in such activities. Perhaps because they enjoyed greater access to such activities, students from wealthier families were more likely than those from poorer families to participate in most student media activities, including student newspapers (13 percent to 10 percent) and Internet publications (9 percent to 5 percent). Unfortunately, access to media-related activities is generally more scarce than it is for so many other activities. Nearly all high schools offer some type of sports program, but far fewer offer media-related activities.

Unlike the case with curricular offerings, student media offerings appear to be on the decline in recent years. As table 2.2 indicates, student media participation has declined in most instances. Only student newspaper participation increased during the two-year period from 2004 to 2006. Meanwhile, participation in other student media activities authorized by the school went down during that same period. Students clearly prefer participation in social-networking sites to participation in school-authorized Internet publications, which declined to just 4 percent in 2006 from 5 percent in 2004.

Table 2.2
Student Participation and Interest in Media-Related
Extracurricular Activities, 2004 and 2006

Media	Participate in 2004	Would Like to Participate (2004)	Participate in 2006
Newspaper	8%	23%	10%
Television	5%	27%	5%
Internet publication	5%	18%	4%
Radio	4%	30%	2%
Magazine	4%	15%	2%
Other media activity	5%	17%	4%

Source: FOFA 2004 and 2006.

The First Line of Defense: Teachers, Principals, and First Amendment Education

In 2004, a clear majority (85 percent) of high school administrators said they wanted to see their schools expand the state of their existing student media programs. Unfortunately, several obstacles cited by these administrators stand in the way of any such expansion. By far, the greatest obstacle cited by the schools, as shown in table 2.3, is the lack of financial resources or budgeting constraints. Another main obstacle, according to administrators, is student apathy or lack of interest in participating in media programs.

Table 2.3
Obstacles Preventing Expansion of Student Media Programs in 2004
(based on 0–10 scale; 0 = not an obstacle; 10 = major obstacle. Average rank shown)

There are not enough financial resources/there are budgeting constraints	8.51
Students are not interested/apathetic	5.14
Teachers lack knowledge to teach/supervise such programs	4.75
This is not an important priority among high school officials	4.60
There is a lack of support from school district officials	4.27
Student media publications are too controversial	3.45

The 2004 survey of high school principals illustrated some of the real problems faced in expanding student media offerings. At the outset, just 33 percent of the principals indicated that they felt it was "very important" that all students learn some journalism skills. And while 72 percent said that school officials were very supportive of students participating in extracurricular activities or clubs, that figure dropped to 29 percent who felt very supportive of the teaching and learning of journalism skills. Clearly, a message is coming from the very top: extracurricular activities as a whole may be important, but that support is not spread evenly to all activities, such as journalism.

Just as surprisingly, more than half (53 percent) of high school principals in 2004 said they personally thought their schools offered "about the right amount" of student media clubs or publications; the exact same percentage said they thought their school offered "about the right amount" of courses primarily dedicated to the teaching of journalism. Obviously, if principals are mostly satisfied, significant expansion of such offerings becomes extremely unlikely.

What about faculty members? Of the nearly eight thousand teachers surveyed in 2004, just 7 percent reported teaching classes that dealt primarily with journalism skills, and less than a quarter (24 percent) reported teaching classes that dealt with the First Amendment. A somewhat larger percentage (42 percent) said they taught classes that discussed the role of media in society.

The 2006 survey indicated just a slight upswing in these numbers. In the later survey, 8 percent of teachers said they taught classes that dealt primarily with journalism skills, 29 percent said they taught classes that dealt with the First Amendment, and 44 percent said they taught classes that dealt with the role of media in society.

How, if at all, are media and journalism issues incorporated in classes? In 2004, 56 percent of the teachers surveyed reported that they required students to read newspapers or watch television news. In 2006, nearly the same percentage (55 percent) of faculty members reported doing so. In 2004, of those who did require such an activity, 48 percent required that students write up reports about what they saw, and 39 percent required that the students give oral presentations in class.

Teacher encouragement of and participation in extracurricular activities also offers an interesting set of findings. In 2004, nearly three in four teachers (73 percent) said they thought it was very important that all students should participate in extracurricular activities; in 2006, 69 percent thought so. And yet, in neither case did that translate into overwhelming support for traditional student media offerings, as only 35 percent of the teachers surveyed in 2004 thought it was very important that all students learn some journalism skills, and just 31 percent of teachers felt that way in 2006.

Not surprisingly, while 56 percent of the teachers reported that they served as coaches for extracurricular clubs or activities, few of them were serving as faculty advisors for student media activities; just 4 percent of the advisors worked with student newspapers, for example.

Apparently, there's not much encouragement coming from the top on these issues. While 70 percent of the teachers surveyed felt that their school's administration was very supportive of student participation in extracurricular activities in general, just one in three felt the administration was very supportive of the teaching and learning of journalism skills. If administrators favor sports activities, one might expect that attitude to result in limited resources for other extracurricular activities, such as student media.

Conclusion

Although modern-day teenagers experience a wide range of influences in their daily lives, schools remain primary agents of political socialization in particular, infusing students' minds with fundamental notions and outlooks on society, government, and laws. Civic education can significantly influence students' political outlooks at a time when they are extremely impressionable. It's a form of education that requires free expression, whether through classroom instruction or extracurricular activities such as student newspapers, and can go a long way toward increasing support for free expression, as well as encouraging students to become appreciative consumers and participants in the marketplace of ideas.

Unfortunately, many schools either are not taking this responsibility to train future democratic citizens seriously or are so financially strapped that they are being forced to leave civic education behind. Student newspapers in particular have become targets of administrative cuts. Although three-quarters of the schools surveyed that offer student media do so in the form of student newspapers, a substantial percentage (40 percent) of those that do not offer student newspapers at their schools say they have been forced to eliminate the activity in recent years. Moreover, an extremely low percentage of students (under 10 percent across the board) indicate that they have participated in student media activities, despite a much greater percentage (raging from 15 percent to 30 percent) expressing some interest in doing so.

As for curricula, while a vast majority of students have used the media for class assignments at some point in their high school careers, more than a third have never taken courses in media and society, and almost three-fourths say they have never taken classes dealing with journalism skills. Nor do teachers or principals offer overwhelming support for traditional student media offerings.

Traditional media was the primary focus of the 2004 survey. In 2006, however, the survey turned its attention to "new" or "digital" media, including social-networking sites, e-mailing, chat groups, and blogging. How does this influx of new media change the equation in the nation's high schools? We explore that subject in greater detail in chapter 4.

Notes

1. Lorraine Smith Pangle and Thomas L. Pangle, "What the American Founders Have to Teach Us about Schooling for Democratic Citizenship," in *Rediscovering the Democratic Purposes of Education*, ed. Lorraine M. McDonnell, P. Michael Timpane, and Roger Benjamin (Lawrence: University Press of Kansas, 2000), 27.

2. John Adams, "A Dissertation on the Canon and Feudal Law," in *The Works of John Adams*, ed. Charles Francis Adams (Boston: Little & Brown, 1851), 448.

3. John C. Fitzpatrick, ed., *The Writings of George Washington from the Original Manuscript Sources* (Washington, DC: Government Printing Office, 1939), 30:493 (cited in Pangle and Pangle, "What the American Founders Have to Teach Us), 43.

4. Pangle and Pangle, "What the American Founders Have to Teach," 25.

    5. Jaroslav Pelikan, "General Introduction: The Public Schools as an Institution of American Constitutional Democracy," in *The Public Schools*, ed. Susan Fuhrman and Marvin Lazerson (New York: Oxford University Press, 2005), xiii–xxi.

    6. Paul Dimond, "School Choice and the Democratic Ideal of Free Schools," in *The Public Schools*, ed. Susan Fuhrman and Marvin Lazerson (New York: Oxford University Press, 2005), 323.

    7. See *Wisconsin v. Yoder*, 406 U.S. 205 (1972).

    8. David Easton and Jack Dennis, *Children in the Political System: Origins of Political Legitimacy* (New York: McGraw-Hill, 1969), 70.

    9. See David Easton, *A Systems Analysis of Political Life* (New York: Wiley & Sons, 1965), ch. 17.

    10. Robert Erikson and Kent Tedin, *American Public Opinion* (New York: Longman, 2001), 116.

    11. Erickson and Tedin, *American Public Opinion*, 116.

    12. Herbert McCloskey and Alida Brill, *Dimensions of Tolerance: What Americans Believe about Civil Liberties* (New York: Russell Sage Foundation, 1983).

    13. McCloskey and Brill, *Dimensions of Tolerance*, 82.

    14. David O. Sears and Nicholas Valentino, "Politics Matters: Political Events as Catalysts for Pre-adult Socialization," *American Political Science Review* 91 (March 1997): 45–64.

    15. Sears and Valentino, "Politics Matters," 59.

    16. M. Kent Jennings and Richard G. Niemi, "Continuity and Change in Political Orientations: A Longitudinal Study of Two Generations," *American Political Science Review* 69 (December 1975), 1316–35.

    17. See Richard Merelman, "Democratic Politics and the Culture of American Education," *American Political Science Review* 74 (1980): 319–32; Kenneth Langton, "Peer Group and School and the Political Process," *American Political Science Review* 61 (1967): 751–58.

    18. Kenneth Langton and M. Kent Jennings, "Political Socialization and the High School Civics Curriculum in the United States," *American Political Science Review* 62 (1968): 852–67.

    19. The landmark work in this regard is V. O. Key Jr., *Public Opinion and American Democracy* (New York: Alfred Knopf, 1963).

    20. Dennis R. Goldenson, "An Alternative View about the Role of Secondary Schools in Political Socialization: A Field-Experimental Study of the Development of Civil Liberties Attitudes," *Theory and Research in Social Education* 6 (1978): 44–72.

    21. Patricia Avery et al., "Exploring Political Tolerance with Adolescents," *Theory and Research in Social Education* 20 (1992): 386–420, 411.

    22. 469 U.S. 325 (1985).

    23. See *Vernonia School District 47J. v. Acton*, 515 U.S. 646 (1995).

    24. See *Board of Curators v. Horowitz*, 435 U.S. 78 (1979); *Regents of University of Michigan v. Ewing*, 474 U.S. 214 (1985).

    25. See *Ingraham v. Wright*, 430 U.S. 651 (1977).

    26. *West Virginia Board of Education v. Barnette*, 319 U.S. 624 (1943).

    27. 393 U.S. 503 (1969).

28. 393 U.S. 503 (1969), 509.

29. 393 U.S. 503 (1969), 506.

30. 478 U.S. 675 (1986).

31. The speech Fraser gave was as follows: "I know a man who is firm—he's firm in his pants, he's firm in his shirt, his character is firm—but most . . . of all, his belief in you, the students of Bethel, is firm. Jeff Kuhlman is a man who takes his point and pounds it in. If necessary, he'll take an issue and nail it to the wall. He doesn't attack things in spurts—he drives hard, pushing and pushing until finally—he succeeds. Jeff is a man who will go to the very end—even the climax, for each and every one of you. So vote for Jeff for A. S. B. vice-president—he'll never come between you and the best our high school can be."

32. 484 U.S. 260 (1988).

33. Id.

34. See Student Press Law Center, "*Hazelwood School District v. Kuhlmeier*: A Complete Guide to the Supreme Court Decision," Student Press Law Center, 1992, 3, www.splc.org/printpage.asp?id=4&tb=legal_research (accessed 1 March 2008).

35. Student Press Law Center, "Student Press Law Center Guide to Surviving Underground," Student Press Law Center, 2001, www.splc.org/legalresearch.asp?id=40 #fn3 (accessed 1 August 2007) (citing "The Tiger Uncaged," 15 Student Press Law Center Report No. 3 [1994], 4, and "Underground Wins Right to Distribute," 17 Student Press Law Center Report No. 1 [Winter 1995–1996], 11).

36. See, e.g., *Lodestar v. Board of Education*, No. B-88-257 (D. Conn, March 10, 1989) (a school publication that was not part of the school's curriculum could not be censored under *Hazelwood*); *Planned Parenthood of Southern Nevada Clark County School District*, 941 F.2d 817 (9th Cir. 1991) (allowing school officials to limit pregnancy-related advertising in a student publication because the publication had never been treated as a public forum).

37. 551 U.S.; 127. S. CT 2618 (2007).

38. See, e.g., the First Amendment Center's reaction to the case in David L. Hudson Jr., "K-12 Public School Student Expression: What's on the Horizon," First Amendment Center, www.firstamendmentcenter.org//speech/studentexpression (accessed 1 March 2008).

39. See, e.g., Jacquelynne S. Eccles and Bonnie Barber, "Student Council, Volunteering, Basketball or Marching Band: What Kind of Extracurricular Involvement Matters?" *Journal of Adolescent Research* 14 (1999): 10–43.

40. Herbert W. Marsh, "Extracurricular Activities: Beneficial Extension of the Traditional Curriculum or Subversion of Academic Goals?" *Journal of Educational Psychology* 84 (1992): 553–62.

41. Joseph Mahoney, "School Extracurricular Activity Participation as a Moderator in the Development of Antisocial Patterns," *Child Development* 71 (2000): 502–16.

42. Joseph Mahoney and Robert Cairns, "Do Extracurricular Activities Protect against Early School Dropout?" *Developmental Psychology* 33 (1997): 241–53.

43. Ralph B. McNeal, "Extracurricular Activities and High School Dropouts," *Sociology of Education* 68 (1995): 62–81.

44. Peter Levine, *The Future of Democracy: Developing the Next Generation of American Citizens* (Medford, MA: Tufts University Press, 2007), 136–40.

45. Michael McDevitt, "The Civic Bonding of School and Family: How Kids Voting Students Enliven the Domestic Sphere" (unpublished report conducted on behalf of the John S. and James L. Knight Foundation, June 6, 2003).

46. Jack Dvorak, "Journalism Student Performance on Advanced Placement Exams," *Journalism and Mass Communication Educator* 53 (1998): 4–12.

47. John Robert Blinn, "A Comparison of Selected Writing Skills of High School Journalism and Non-Journalism Students" (unpublished PhD diss., Ohio University, 1992).

48. Dorothy McPhillips, "ACT Research Report Validates Journalism in the Curriculum," *NASSP Bulletin* 72 (1998): 11–16.

3

The School Curriculum, Student Media, and Attitudes about Freedom of Expression

IN CHAPTER 2 WE EXAMINED THE ROLE of the secondary school system in fostering an appreciation for freedom of expression. As agents of socialization, the schools play a large role in promoting the values of free expression. In fact, an important argument in the development of free public education featured the goal of developing citizenship skills. We hypothesized that an educational curriculum including instruction on the First Amendment, the role of the media in society, and journalism skills should favorably influence students' appreciation for and attitudes toward free expression rights. We also reported in chapter 2 that a large and growing number of students are now taking classes with relevant content. In 2006, 72 percent of high school students claimed that they had taken at least one high school class that dealt with the First Amendment, which represented a fourteen-percentage-point increase over a two-year period. During the same period, we noted a ten-percentage-point increase, to 62 percent, in the number of students taking classes that discussed the role of media in society. In 2006, 26 percent said they had taken a high school class that dealt primarily with journalism skills, up five points. Given that the preponderance of students is receiving instruction in these areas, the potential for a positive classroom influence on free expression rights is certainly a possibility.

We also hypothesized that, in addition to course work and instruction, certain extracurricular activities may produce more favorable perspectives toward free expression rights. Specifically, extracurricular activities that engage students in expressive activities, where free speech and free press rights apply to their work, might help develop a more positive appreciation for free expression rights. These extracurricular activities include student work and participation in media activities, including the school newspaper, school Web news site, school TV, or other school news publications. Certainly, the number of students participating in school media extracurricular activities is smaller than the number of students who receive classroom instruction. Specifically, in 2006, only 10 percent reported being involved in the school newspapers, 5 percent in a school TV station, 4 percent in a school Web publication, and 2 percent each in radio and magazine activities. These smaller numbers are in part the result of schools offering few of these activities. Also, as table 3.1 indicates, student media opportunities are not universally offered in schools across the country. In fact, one in five schools offer no student media whatsoever.

Table 3.1
Media Activities Offered in
U.S. High Schools, 2004

No media offered	21%
One media activity offered	51%
Two or more activities	18%
Four or more activities	10%
Offers student newspaper	74%
Offers school Internet publication	21%
Offers student-run TV	14%
Offers student magazine	7%
Offers student-run radio	3%

Source: FOFA 2004 (Administrators' survey).

A look at the relationship between the media curriculum and student academic performance suggests that students who get First Amendment instruction and classes on the role of the media in society perform better academically than students who do not receive this type of instruction. For example, our study found that 77 percent of students who have had First Amendment instruction report having either an A (32 percent) or B (45 percent) overall grade average. In contrast, 71 percent of those who have not had a course with First Amendment content report having an A (28 percent) or B (43 percent) average. Also, 78 percent of students who have learned about the media and society report having an A or B average, compared to 71 percent who have not had such course work. Corroborating the findings from Jack Dvorak's prior research,[1] the extracurricular experience of working on a school newspaper is also related to academic average: 81 percent of those on the student newspaper report an A or B average, while 75 percent of those who did not participate in student newspapers have at least a B average.

While exposure to First Amendment and media course work, along with student newspaper experiences, helps to lay the groundwork for better academic performance, does it also say the groundwork for building more positive attitudes and orientations toward free expression? In this chapter, we explore the relationship between the First Amendment, media, and the journalism curriculum on the one hand and attitudes about free expression rights on the other. Does education both in and out of the classroom matter? We also examine the experiential effects of utilizing free expression rights in the form of extracurricular activities on attitudes about free expression rights.

Data Analysis

In the sections of this chapter that follow, data from the Future of the First Amendment (FOFA) 2006 survey are used in the analysis. We constructed a number of "independent variables" to facilitate an examination of the relationships between (1) the high school First Amendment/media/journalism curriculum and attitudes about free expression rights, and (2) the high school extracurricular activities that deal with student media and attitudes about free expression rights. The following represents how we constructed these two sets of independent variables.

Curriculum Variables

Students were asked three questions to determine their exposure to classes with particular types of content. These questions produced the following variables:

1. First Amendment classes: "Have you ever taken classes in high school that dealt with the First Amendment to the U.S. Constitution?" Those answering yes included 72 percent of all students, and those saying no amounted to 28 percent.
2. Media in society classes: "Have you ever taken classes in high school that discuss the role of the media in society?" Those answering yes were 62 percent, and no responses were 38 percent.
3. Journalism skills classes: "Have you ever taken classes in high school that dealt primarily with journalism skills?" Twenty-six percent answered yes, and 74 percent said no.

Extracurricular Student Media

Students were asked the following on the FOFA 2006 survey: "Please indicate whether or not you have been involved in any of the following activities at your high school." The list included student newspaper, student magazine with a news component (and not including literary magazines or yearbook), student-run radio station with a news component, student-run television station with a news component, and student Internet publication with a news component. The following variables were created from this item set:

1. Student newspaper participation, with the categories (1) participant (10 percent of all students surveyed), and (2) nonparticipant (90 percent of students)
2. Student news magazine participation, with the categories (1) participant (2 percent of all students), and (2) nonparticipant (98 percent)
3. Student radio news participation, with the categories (1) participant (2 percent of all students), and (2) nonparticipant (98 percent)
4. Student news television participation, with the categories (1) participant (5 percent of all students), and (2) nonparticipant (95 percent)
5. Student Internet publication participation, with the categories (1) participant (5 percent of students), and (2) nonparticipant (95 percent)

Are Students Who Get Curricular and/or Extracurricular Experiences More Attentive to News?

Student interest in following news and current events tends to be lukewarm at best. Only 4 percent of students say they are "extremely" interested in following the news, and another 17 percent report being "very" interested. The vast majority, 70 percent, say they are "somewhat" interested in following the news, with 10 percent admitting that they are "not" interested in following news and current events.

As shown in column 1 of table 3.2, without controlling for any confounding factors, there appears to be a link between interest in following the news and specific courses that emphasize issues related to the First Amendment. Even though overall levels of interest are low, high school students who take courses that deal with the First Amendment, journalism, and issues relating to the media and society tend to be more interested in following news and current events, indicating that these curricular items inspire an attentiveness to the news environment. Specifically, 22 percent of students who have taken classes with First Amendment content report being either very or extremely interested in following news and current events, compared to 16 percent of those who have had no such instruction. Similarly, 23 percent of those who have taken classes on the role of the media in society are at least very interested in the news, compared to 16 percent

Table 3.2

Interest in Following the News and Current Events and School Curriculum and Extracurricular Activities with News Content, 2006

	Unadjusted (%)	Adjusted (%)
School Curriculum		
Class in high school that dealt with the First Amendment to the U.S. Constitution		
Had taken	22	19
Had never taken	16	17
Difference (in percentage points)	6*	2*
Class in high school that dealt with the role of media in society		
Had taken	23	20
Had never taken	16	17
Difference (in percentage points)	7*	3*
Class in high school that dealt primarily with journalism skills		
Had taken	24	19
Had never taken	19	18
Difference (in percentage points)	5*	1
Extracurricular Activities with News Content		
Student newspaper		
Participated	33	25
Did not participate	19	18
Difference (in percentage points)	13*	7*
School magazine		
Participated	32	20
Did not participate	20	18
Difference (in percentage points)	12*	8
School radio		
Participated	25	15

(continued)

Table 3.2 *(continued)*

	Unadjusted (%)	Adjusted (%)
Did not participate	21	19
Difference (in percentage points)	4*	-4
School TV station		
Participated	29	20
Did not participate	20	18
Difference (in percentage points)	9*	2
School Internet site		
Participated	32	21
Did not participate	20	18
Difference (in percentage points)	12*	3

Source: FOFA 2006. Adjusted percentages are obtained from a probit model that controls for participation in specific courses, extracurricular activities with news content, use of the Internet for news consumption, and other factors such as gender, race or ethnicity, school type, self-reported GPA, type of Internet access, U.S. citizenship, self-reported economic class, and grade enrolled in at the time of the survey. For complete probit results, see appendix C, table C.1. An * indicates that the difference is statistically significant at the 5 percent level.

of students who have not had this course. Finally, 24 percent of those who have had a course focusing on journalism skills, as opposed to 19 percent of those without this type of class, express a high interest in the news.

Certainly, some of these observed differences may be due to factors other than whether or not a student has taken a course that emphasizes the importance of the First Amendment. In order to address this issue, we estimated a multivariate model to explain interest in following the news and current events among 2006 FOFA participants. Factors that we are able to control include measures of participation in extracurricular activities that have news content, Internet usage, and demographic measures such as gender, race or ethnicity, economic class, school type, and self-reported grade point average. Probit model full results for this model are shown in appendix C, table C.1.

As table 3.2 shows, after adjusting for many observed background, and potentially confounding, factors, we find that many of the large differences between students who take specific courses in the school curriculum and those who do not are reduced, though two of three factors remain statistically significant. For example, students who take a course that emphasizes the First Amendment are still more likely to be "very" or "extremely" interested in following the news or current events by a statistically significant margin of two percentage points. Furthermore, of students who had taken a media class, 20 percent said they were interested in following the news or current events, while 17 percent of those who had not taken a media class answered similarly, by a statistically significant difference of three percentage points.

As column 1 of table 3.2 shows, engagement in high school extracurricular media activities, without controlling for confounding factors, appears to have a very strong relationship with interest in following current events. Nearly one-third of students who participate in the school newspaper (33 percent), the school magazine (32 percent), or a school Internet news site (32 percent) are at least very interested in the news, compared to one-fifth (19 percent) of students who do not participate in any student media activity. School TV station (29 percent) and radio station (25 percent) participants also register higher levels of interest in news and current events. As expected, the experience of actually working in a medium in a school setting bears a very strong relationship to interest in the news.

As before, there may be factors that confound the effect of participation in student extracurricular news activities and interest in following the news and current events. Column 2 of table 3.2 presents results adjusted for many confounding factors. Once these factors are controlled, students who participated in student newspapers show a statistically significant seven-point increase in interest in the news compared with students who did not participate in a student newspaper.

Are Students Who Get Curricular Instruction
More Supportive of Freedom of Expression?

Several sets of survey items were used to measure support for free expression rights. One general item, which we reported on in chapter 1, was borrowed from the Freedom Forum State of the First Amendment (SOFA) surveys:

> The First Amendment became part of the U.S. Constitution more than 200 years ago. This is what it says: "Congress shall make no law respecting an establishment of religion or prohibiting the free exercise thereof, or abridging the freedom of speech or the press, or the right of the people to peaceably assemble, and to petition the government for a redress of grievances." Based on your own feelings about the First Amendment, please tell me whether you agree or disagree with the following statement: The First Amendment goes too far in the rights it guarantees.

In the FOFA 2006 survey, 45 percent of high school students agreed (18 percent strongly agreed and another 27 percent mildly agreed) that the First Amendment goes too far in the rights it guarantees, while 37 percent disagreed (21 percent strongly and 16 percent mildly). Fully 19 percent of students said they did not know enough to offer an opinion.

An interesting relationship between course content and attitudes about whether the First Amendment goes too far emerges. First, as table 3.3 shows, students who have taken classes either with First Amendment content or that address the role of the media in society are less likely to offer "no opinion" as a response to this question. Of those who have had such courses, 16 percent offer no opinion, while one-quarter of those without these classes say they don't know, a statistically significant difference. This indicates that instruction on the First Amendment and the role of the media in society may relate to student attitude development and formation. Interestingly, however, students who take classes dealing with journalism skills development are no more likely to have an opinion on whether the First Amendment goes too far than students who did not take these classes. If anything, this suggests that a skills-based journalism course, while perhaps advancing student skills in that area, does not produce a broader affinity for the First Amendment per se.

Among those who have taken a class with First Amendment content, 39 percent disagree that the First Amendment goes too far in the rights it guarantees, while 45 percent agree, which represents a statistically significant six-percentage-point difference. In contrast, among those who have not taken such a class, 30 percent disagree, while 44 percent agree, which represents a larger fourteen-percentage-point marginal difference. A similar relationship is found with respect to class content on the role of the media in society. Among those who have taken these classes, 39 percent disagree that the First Amendment goes too

Table 3.3

Views of the First Amendment and School Curriculum and Extracurricular Activities with News Content, 2006

| | Does the First Amendment Go Too Far in the Rights It Guarantees? | | | | | |
| | Agree | | Disagree | | No Opinion | |
	Unadjusted (%)	Adjusted (%)	Unadjusted (%)	Adjusted (%)	Unadjusted (%)	Adjusted (%)
School Curriculum						
Class in high school that dealt with the First Amendment to the U.S. Constitution						
Had taken	45	47	39	37	16	16
Had never taken	44	45	30	34	26	21
Difference (in percentage points)	1	2	9*	3	-10*	-5*
Class in high school that dealt with the role of media in society						
Had taken	45	47	39	37	16	16
Had never taken	44	46	32	34	24	20
Difference (in percentage points)	1	1	7*	3	-8*	-4*
Class in high school that dealt primarily with journalism skills						
Had taken	50	51	32	36	19	17
Had never taken	43	45	38	38	19	17
Difference (in percentage points)	7*	6*	-6*	-2*	0	0

Source: FOFA 2006. Adjusted percentages are obtained from a multinomial logit model that controls for participation in specific courses, extracurricular activities with news content, use of the Internet for news consumption, and other factors such as gender, race or ethnicity, school type, self-reported GPA, type of Internet access, U.S. citizenship, self-reported economic class, and grade enrolled in at the time of the survey. For complete multinomial logit results, see appendix C, table C.2. An * indicates that the difference is statistically significant at the 95 percent level.

far, while 45 percent agree, which indicates a statistically significant six-percentage-point difference. In comparison, of those who have not taken a media and society class, 32 percent disagree, and 44 percent agree, a twelve-percentage-point difference.

Once again, in order to control for confounding factors, we also adjusted the percentages shown above by estimating a multivariate model that controls for many other factors.[2] Once these factors are controlled, the observed differences between those who participated in a specific part of a high school curriculum and those who did not remain statistically significant. For example, the difference between those who took a First Amendment course and a media course and those who did not is reduced by half, though it continues to be statistically significant. These findings suggest not only that learning and attitude development do occur as a result of First Amendment and media and society classroom instruction but also that the attitude formation that does occur moves students in a more favorable, pro–First Amendment direction; that is, these students are more prone to disagree that the rights embedded in the First Amendment go too far. In addition, however, we find that journalism skills–based classes do not seem to promote attitude development, though among those who have formed an opinion, it is slightly more positive if the student has taken a course emphasizing journalism skills.

Does the Press Have Excessive Freedom in America?

A second item on the survey specifically focuses on freedom of the press. It asks, "Overall, do you think the press in America has too much freedom to do what it wants, too little freedom to do what it wants, or is the amount of freedom the press has about right?" Among all high school students, 41 percent say that the press has the right amount of freedom, while 30 percent say it has too much, and 11 percent say it has too little freedom. Nearly one-fifth (18 percent) of students say they do not know enough about this to have an opinion.

As table 3.4 shows, when comparing responses of those who have had First Amendment, media and society, and journalism skills classes with those who have not had such classes, the same pattern emerges: classes dealing with the concepts of the First Amendment and the role of the media in society seems to promote the formation of opinions about the press's level of freedom, while the journalism skills–based classes do not. Also, students who have had this classroom instruction are more likely to say that the press has "the right amount" of freedom than those who have not had this type of instruction. Many of these differences, while reduced, are still prevalent once confounding background factors are controlled.

Table 3.4

Views of Press Freedom in America and School Curriculum, 2006

	Overall, Does the Press in America Have . . .							
	Too Much Freedom		Too Little Freedom		About Right		Don't Know	
	Unadjusted (%)	Adjusted (%)	Unadjusted (%)	Adjusted (%)	Unadjusted (%)	Adjusted (%)	Unadjusted (%)	Adjusted (%)
Class in high school that dealt with the First Amendment to the U.S. Constitution								
Had taken	30	31	11	11	42	42	16	16
Had never taken	28	29	11	11	38	41	23	18
Difference (in percentage points)	2*	2	0	0	6*	1	7*	−2*
Class in high school that dealt with the role of media in society								
Had taken	30	30	11	10	43	44	15	15
Had never taken	29	30	12	11	37	40	22	19
Difference (in percentage points)	1*	0	−1	−1	6*	4	−7*	−4*
Class in high school that dealt primarily with journalism skills								
Had taken	26	28	14	12	40	41	18	19
Had never taken	31	31	10	10	41	42	19	16
Difference (in percentage points)	−5*	−3	4*	2*	−1	−1	−1	3*

Source: FOFA 2006. Adjusted percentages are obtained from a multinomial logit model that controls for participation in specific courses, extracurricular activities with news content, use of the Internet for news consumption, and other factors such as gender, race or ethnicity, school type, self-reported GPA, type of Internet access, U.S. citizenship, self-reported economic class, and grade enrolled in at the time of the survey. For complete multinomial logit results, see appendix C, table C.3. An * indicates that the difference is statistically significant at the 5 percent level.

The Dimensions of Free Expression

A third method of querying students required interviewers first to read a set of statements featuring the exercise of free expression rights, then to ask respondents to agree or disagree with each statement. These are the five statements used:

1. People should be allowed to express unpopular opinions.
2. People should be allowed to burn or deface the American flag as a political statement.
3. Musicians should be allowed to sing songs with lyrics that others might find offensive.
4. Newspapers should be allowed to publish freely without government approval of a story.
5. High school students should be allowed to report controversial issues in their student newspapers without the approval of school authorities.

These five statements tap into students' attitudes on a number of dimensions. Items 1 and 2 offer a more general, abstract notion of the right to expression (item 1), followed by a concrete, specific example (item 2). Statement 4 depicts a traditional framework that has been used to support free expression rights, while statement 3 provides an alternative framework that might help students to think about expression rights more "outside the box." Statements 5 and 3 both encourage students to think about how expression rights might affect them more directly, while the other items are less self-directed. Together, these items present an array of dimensions with which to tap student attitudes toward the rights of free expression.

Table 3.5 presents the findings on these five survey items overall, then broken down by the First Amendment, media and society, and journalism skills class work groupings. The table shows that overall, at the broader, abstract level, the vast majority of high school students give free expression rights a high degree of support. For example, 85 percent say that people should be able to express unpopular opinions. However, when it comes to a concrete example of unpopular speech, like flag burning, support for expression drops off quite a bit, with only 15 percent saying that people should be allowed to do this. These findings of higher support for the broad concepts of free expression and lower support for concrete concepts support the findings presented earlier by Prothro and Grigg (1960), Stouffer (1955), McCloskey and Brill (1983), and Yalof and Dautrich (2002). Indeed, students exhibit the same pattern of support for expression rights at the abstract and concrete levels.

The overall findings also suggest that when free expression rights issues are brought closer to home, students respond more favorably in support of the rights. For example, while 55 percent of students agree that newspapers should

Table 3.5
Views of Press Freedom in America and School Curriculum, 2006

First Amendment Attitudes

(%)	Unpopular Opinions (1)		Flag Burning (2)		Offensive Song Lyrics (3)		Papers Publishing Freely (4)		Student Paper Issues (5)	
	Unadjusted (%)	*Adjusted (%)*	*Unadjusted (%)*	*Adjusted (%)*	*Unadjusted (%)*	*Adjusted (%)*	*Unadjusted (%)*	*Adjusted (%)*	*Unadjusted (%)*	*Adjusted (%)*
All high schoolers										
Agree	85	88	15	15	69	70	55	55	64	66
Disagree	7	6	76	78	23	23	35	36	25	25
No opinion	7	6	8	7	8	6	10	9	11	9
Taken First Amendment class										
Agree	88	88	16	15	70	71	55	55	65	65
Disagree	6	6	77	78	23	23	36	37	25	26
No opinion	6	5	7	7	7	6	9	8	9	9
Not taken First Amendment class										
Agree	82	87	14	14	65	70	51	55	61	67
Disagree	8	7	76	77	25	23	35	34	23	23
No opinion	10	6	11	9	10	8	14	11	15	11
Taken media/ society class										
Agree	89	89	16	15	71	72	56	56	67	67
Disagree	6	6	77	79	22	22	36	36	25	25
No opinion	5	5	7	7	6	6	8	8	8	8

(continued)

Table 3.5 (continued)

First Amendment Attitudes

(%)	Unpopular Opinions (1)		Flag Burning (2)		Offensive Song Lyrics (3)		Papers Publishing Freely (4)		Student Paper Issues (5)	
	Unadjusted (%)	Adjusted (%)	Unadjusted (%)	Adjusted (%)	Unadjusted (%)	Adjusted (%)	Unadjusted (%)	Adjusted (%)	Unadjusted (%)	Adjusted (%)
Not taken media/ society class										
Agree	81	85	14	14	65	68	51	53	60	63
Disagree	8	7	75	78	25	24	35	36	25	25
No opinion	10	7	10	8	10	8	14	11	15	11
Taken journalism class										
Agree	84	86	19	14	67	68	54	53	64	63
Disagree	8	8	73	78	25	25	35	36	26	27
No opinion	7	6	8	7	8	7	11	11	11	10
Not taken journalism class										
Agree	86	89	15	15	69	71	54	55	64	66
Disagree	6	6	77	76	23	22	36	36	25	25
No opinion	7	5	8	9	8	6	10	8	11	9

Source: FOFA 2006. Adjusted percentages are obtained from a multinomial logit model that controls for participation in specific courses, extracurricular activities with news content, use of the Internet for news consumption, and other factors such as gender, race or ethnicity, school type, self-reported GPA, type of Internet access, U.S. citizenship, self-reported economic class, and grade enrolled in at the time of the survey. For complete multinomial logit results, see appendix C, tables C.6 to C.10.

be allowed to publish without government approval of a story, as many as 65 percent agree that high school students should be allowed to report controversial issues in their school newspapers without the approval of school authorities. Further, when it comes to the right of musicians to sing songs with lyrics that might be offensive to some, fully 69 percent of students support the musicians' right of free expression.

Table 3.5 also depicts the relationship between class content and support for these various dimensions of expression rights, with both raw unadjusted differences and adjusted differences. The data convincingly support the findings for the more general First Amendment and "press freedom" survey items presented earlier. Specifically, the table shows, even when confounding factors are controlled, that (1) those students who have taken courses that include First Amendment or media and society content are more likely to have formulated opinions about free expression situations, (2) those students who have taken skills-based journalism courses are not more likely to have formulated such opinions, and (3) the opinion formation appears to contribute generally toward greater support for the rights of free expression.

For example, 9 percent of those who have taken a course with First Amendment content do not express an opinion on item 4, while 14 percent of those without First Amendment instruction express no opinion, a statistically significant difference. Once confounding factors are controlled, this difference is reduced to a statistically significant three percentage points, with 8 percent of those who have taken a course with First Amendment content offering no opinion, while 11 percent of their counterparts fail to do so. For items 2, 3, and 5, the respective unadjusted differences are 7 percent and 11 percent, 7 percent and 10 percent, and 9 percent and 15 percent (all statistically significant). The same pattern holds true for those receiving media and society instruction for all five items: those who have had instruction are more likely to have a formed opinion, with many differences being statistically significant but slightly mitigated as confounding factors are controlled. However, those who have taken journalism skills courses are not any more likely to have a formed opinion on the propriety of free speech expression. Furthermore, in some cases, as with item 4, once adjusted for confounding factors, those who have taken a journalism skills class are less likely to have formed an opinion than those who have not taken a journalism skills class, and the difference is statistically significant.

In addition, in most cases the difference between those agreeing and those disagreeing with the expression right increases among those who have had the class content. For example, on item 3, the difference between agreement and disagreement on whether a musician should be allowed to sing songs with offensive lyrics among those taking a First Amendment class is plus forty-seven percentage points (70–23), while the same difference among those not taking a First Amendment class is plus forty percentage points (65–25). Similarly, the difference between media and society class takers on item 5 is plus forty-two, while it is plus thirty-five for those who have not taken a media and society class. While the magnitude of the differences between class takers varies, the pattern across the items remains the same: those taking classes with First Amendment and media and society content are more likely to agree with the right to expression under varying circumstances.

A final set of survey items approaches student orientations toward the First Amendment by asking about the extent to which it is taken for granted. Free expression is a fundamental liberty that underlies the very roots of American democracy. Free speech and free press rights were not new at the time the Constitution was written; rather, they were already part and parcel of the mechanics of government. Since these rights have existed for so long, an important question that arises is whether we as a society are so accustomed to having free expression rights that we now may be taking those rights for granted. Our survey of high school students included two items that tapped this concept: "Do you agree or disagree with the following statement: Americans don't appreciate First Amendment freedoms the way they ought to?" and "Are the rights guaranteed by the First Amendment something you personally think about or are they something that you take for granted?"

Overall, when it comes to students' self-assessment, only 24 percent say that the First Amendment is something that they personally think about, and 42 percent admit that it is something that they take for granted. Another 34 percent offer no opinion on this question, indicating that for the vast majority of high school students, there is not much consideration of the significance of free expression rights. When it comes to thinking about others' appreciation for the First Amendment, 53 percent agree that Americans do not appreciate the First Amendment they way they ought to, and 24 percent disagree with this. Fully 22 percent offer no opinion.

The survey of students does find that First Amendment and media and society course work both share a relationship with the self-assessment item. Those who took First Amendment classes are statistically more likely to say that they personally think about these rights (26 percent compared to 19 percent of those with no classes), and they are more likely to have a formed an opinion on this by a margin of twelve percentage points. Similarly, 27 percent of those with media and society instruction personally think about the First Amendment, compared to 20 percent of those with no classes, and class takers are eleven points more likely to have a formed opinion. Both of these differences remain once other observed factors are controlled.[3]

In the general assessment of whether Americans take their rights for granted, both those who have taken First Amendment and media and society classes are ten points (statistically significant) more likely than those without instruction to have formed attitudes, again confirming that classes on these topics do promote the development and formation of attitudes. In this case, however, the instruction encourages the formation of student attitudes that suggest Americans are even less appreciative of the First Amendment than they ought to be. That is, 56 percent of students with First Amendment class instruction agree that Americans do not appreciate their rights the way they ought to, while 47 percent of those without instruction feel that way. Also, 56 percent of students who have media and society classes feel that Americans don't appreciate their free expression rights compared to 49 percent of students without such classes, a statistically significant difference.

Are Students Who Participate in School Media Activities More Supportive of the First Amendment?

In examining the relationship between participation in student media activities and attitudes about free expression, we again use the FOFA 2006 student survey data. We compare students who participate in (1) the student newspaper, (2) the school TV station, and (3) the school Web news site versus nonparticipants across the survey items that tap free expression attitudes.[4]

Does the First Amendment Go Too Far in the Rights It Guarantees?

Earlier, we demonstrated that students who have taken a class with First Amendment or media and society content tend to have better-developed attitudes on the issue of whether the First Amendment goes too far in the rights it guarantees. Students taking these classes are also more likely to express pro–First Amendment opinions on this topic, even after confounding factors are controlled. With respect to student media activities, the data indicate that both of these dynamics hold true for school newspaper participants. Those involved with newspapers are statistically more likely to hold an opinion than are nonparticipants (13 percent no opinion versus 20 percent); they are also more likely to disagree (by six points) that the First Amendment goes too far in the rights that it guarantees. For student TV and Web activities, we do find some evidence of attitude formation. TV students are four points more likely to offer an opinion, and Web students are six points more likely, though once confounding factors are controlled, these differences are eliminated. However, there is no evidence of a positive effect on pro–free expression positions whether confounding factors are controlled or not.[5]

Does the Press in America Have Excessive Freedom?

On the item directed specifically at press freedoms,[6] we find attitude formation in a direction that favors press freedoms in evidence among participants in all three media activities. Newspaper, TV, and Web participation reduces "no opinion" responses to this item by six points, three points, and four points, respectively; it increases the percentage saying that "the press has too little freedom to do what it wants" by six points, six points, and seven points, respectively. However, once confounding factors are controlled, positive attitude formation toward the First Amendment remains only for students who participate in student newspapers.[7] The findings suggest that student experiential learning in newspaper activities has a formative and positive influence on opinions about the expansion of press freedoms, while other media experiences do not necessarily produce such effects.

The Dimensions of Free Expression

Table 3.6 shows the five statements of free speech expression examined by student media participation. Generally, the table suggests that student media experiences do not significantly enhance the formation of attitudes from nonopinions, as was detected in table 3.5 (showing the correlation of course content in First Amendment or media and society with these five items). In fact, the lack of a relationship between the student media experience and the expression of an opinion on items 1 to 5 is similar to the lack of such a relationship between journalism skills instruction and items 1 to 5. This finding reinforces the idea that skills-based education, whether it be in the form of a journalism skills class or practicing journalism through a student media activity, does not necessarily serve to help students formulate opinions on free expression issues when such opinions were nonexistent before the skills-based journalism experience.

Table 3.6 does, however, depict a relationship between school newspaper involvement and four of the five free expression scenarios. Newspaper participants are ten points more likely to agree that flag burning should be allowed and ten points more likely to agree that newspapers should be allowed to publish freely without government approval of a story; these differences remain largely unchanged as confounding factors are controlled. School newspaper students are also eight points more likely to agree that students should be allowed to report controversial issues without administrative approval and four points more apt to say that musicians should be allowed to sing songs with potentially offensive lyrics. Only on the most abstract item (item 1), where

Table 3.6

Views of Press Freedom in America and Participation in Extracurricular Activities with News Content, 2006

First Amendment Attitudes

(%)	Unpopular Opinions		Flag Burning		Offensive Song Lyrics		Papers Publishing Freely		Student Paper Issues	
	Unadjusted (%)	Adjusted (%)	Unadjusted (%)	Adjusted (%)	Unadjusted (%)	Adjusted (%)	Unadjusted (%)	Adjusted (%)	Unadjusted (%)	Adjusted (%)
Newspaper participant										
Agree	88	89	25	20	72	74	63	63	71	71
Disagree	7	6	68	74	22	21	30	31	22	21
No opinion	5	5	7	6	6	5	8	7	8	8
Not newspaper participant										
Agree	86	88	15	14	68	70	53	54	63	65
Disagree	7	6	78	79	23	23	36	37	25	26
No opinion	8	6	8	7	8	7	11	9	11	10
TV participant										
Agree	85	87	23	14	70	71	59	58	70	69
Disagree	9	7	67	77	22	21	31	33	22	22
No opinion	6	6	9	9	7	7	10	9	9	8
Not TV participant										
Agree	86	88	16	14	69	70	54	55	63	65
Disagree	7	6	76	78	23	23	36	36	25	25
No opinion	7	6	8	7	8	6	10	9	11	9

(continued)

Table 3.6 (continued)

First Amendment Attitudes

(%)	Unpopular Opinions		Flag Burning		Offensive Song Lyrics		Papers Publishing Freely		Student Paper Issues	
	Unadjusted (%)	Adjusted (%)	Unadjusted (%)	Adjusted (%)	Unadjusted (%)	Adjusted (%)	Unadjusted (%)	Adjusted (%)	Unadjusted (%)	Adjusted (%)
Web participant										
Agree	85	87	25	14	66	66	55	50	64	62
Disagree	11	9	65	77	28	28	34	40	24	28
No opinion	4	4	9	9	6	5	11	11	11	12
Not Web participant										
Agree	86	88	16	15	69	70	55	55	64	66
Disagree	7	6	76	78	23	23	36	36	25	25
No opinion	8	6	8	7	8	7	10	9	11	9

Source: FOFA 2006. Adjusted percentages are obtained from a multinomial logit model that controls for participation in specific courses, extracurricular activities with news content, use of the Internet for news consumption, and other factors such as gender, race or ethnicity, school type, self-reported GPA, type of Internet access, U.S. citizenship, self-reported economic class, and grade enrolled in at the time of the survey. For complete multinomial logit results, see appendix C, tables C.6 to C.10.

agreement is very high, does newspaper participation bear no statistically detectable relationship to the direction of opinion, even when adjusted for confounding factors.

Student TV media experience shares a statistical relationship with three of the five free expression scenarios: TV students are seven points more likely to say that students should be able to publish without school-authority consent, and they are three points more likely to agree that newspapers should be able to publish without government approval, with both differences still present once confounding factors are controlled. For school Web students, the only difference is on the flag burning issue, where Web participants favor the free expression of opinions by nine more percentage points, though this difference is eliminated once confounding factors are controlled.

The positive impact of school media activity on opinions about free expression appears less pronounced than the influence of courses that focus on the conceptual content of First Amendment rights and the role of the media in our society. To be sure, student newspaper participation does bear on proexpression rights in most scenarios. The relationship between TV activities, particularly Web-based activities, is less apparent. In addition, student media participation appears to contribute less to creating and helping to formulate opinions on free expression rights than it does to affecting the positive direction of opinions.

What about the differences between media and nonmedia activities and their influence on taking First Amendment rights for granted? School newspaper students, school TV students, and school Web students each report marginally higher rates of four percentage points in how much they personally think about the rights guaranteed by the First Amendment. And by seven points, newspaper students are more likely than non–newspaper students to agree that Americans do not appreciate the First Amendment's free expression rights as they ought to.

Conclusion and Discussion

High schools in America are pulled in many different directions. Political leaders, parents, employers, and the public expect them to teach the "three R's," to prepare students for college, to promote success in standardized testing, to advance education in math and science, to promote technological literacy, and to encourage an appreciation for the arts, literature, and diversity. The roots of public education also suggest that schools should be socializing students to appreciate core American democratic values and to become capable citizens contributing to self-government. The schools are expected to accomplish many things, including the focus of this book: providing the citizenship skills related to free expression rights.

High school students who take classes that include content dealing with the First Amendment more closely follow news. Likewise, students who take a First Amendment class or one on the media in society have better developed opinions about the importance of free expression rights in our democracy. They are also consistently more supportive of pro–First Amendment positions across a variety of topics and situations. Further, students who take these classes are more likely to feel that the press is afforded the appropriate amount of freedom to do its job effectively. In short, classes that pursue topics related to the First Amendment and the media in society do have a positive influence on student orientations toward the First Amendment. The research also indicates that student participation in extracurricular school media activities is also valuable in engendering positive orientations toward free expression rights. This is particularly true of student contributions to the school newspaper.

The high schools' endeavors with respect to First Amendment classes, media and society classes, and student media activities relate positively to student support for the First Amendment. The larger question, however, is, are the schools doing enough? Given the crowded agenda of the nation's high schools, are enough courses, programs, and activities available to students for the educational system to effectively socialize them in the values of free expression in our society? Is there enough focus to ensure the future vitality of free expression rights?

Unfortunately, the nation's high schools are generally not engaged in finding new and innovative ways to expand their curricula on the First Amendment. While there are some major private and foundation initiatives, such as the Freedom Forum's First Amendment Schools and the Knight Foundation's J-Ideas, as well as other high school journalism initiatives, policy makers and administrators at the state and local levels are more focused on other agendas, most notably the standards promulgated by No Child Left Behind test scoring. In addition, school budgets are stretched to their limits. More than any other factor, high school principals report that budget constraints are the single biggest factor precluding them from increasing their schools' focus on the First Amendment.

As a result, student journalism has yet to become a fixture in the high school curriculum in most schools. While about three-quarters of the high schools offer a student newspaper as an extracurricular activity, other student media activities are sparsely offered. Moreover, among the schools that do not offer a student newspaper, as many as 40 percent have dropped their student paper within the last five years. Today, about one in ten students reports having participated in his or her school student newspaper, and less than one in twenty reports participating in another news-based student media activity.

Meanwhile, the student demand to participate in a student media activity remains high, despite the trend toward reduced offerings.

On a more positive note, the number of students who report having taken a class that deals with First Amendment material is on the upswing (from 58 percent in 2004 to 72 percent in 2006). But while a clear majority of students have received at least some First Amendment instruction, still nearly three in ten report not having any class work on free expression rights, nearly four in ten have had nothing on the role of the media in society, and three-quarters have had no classes that teach journalism skills.

American high schools do have classes and programs that promote First Amendment appreciation and support for free expression rights, but there are not enough of them. Perhaps the future of the First Amendment would be better served by a renewed effort to invoke more First Amendment instruction and student media opportunities for American high school students.

Notes

1. See, e.g., Jack Dvorak, "Journalism Student Performance on Advanced Placement Exams," *Journalism and Mass Communication Educator* 53 (1998): 4–12.

2. See appendix C, table C.2 for the full multinomial logit results used to generate the adjusted percentages in table 4.2.

3. See appendix C, table C.5 for full multinomial logit model results used to generate adjusted differences.

4. In the 2006 Knight Foundation survey of 14,500 students, a total of 1,450 reported being involved in the school newspaper, 722 in school TV news activity, and 556 in a school Web activity with news content. These groups provide adequate sample sizes for comparison with nonparticipants in school media activities. We do not report on student radio participants due to the lower subsample size of that group ($n = 249$).

5. See appendix C, table C.2 for complete multinomial logit results used to generate adjusted percentages.

6. This item reads, "Overall, do you think the press in America has too much freedom to do what it wants, too little freedom to do what it wants, or is the amount of freedom the press has about right?"

7. See appendix C, table C.3 for complete multinomial logit results used to generate adjusted percentages.

4

The Invasion of the Bloggers: Coming to a High School Near You

Libertyville High School Confronts the Digital Age

LIBERTYVILLE, ILLINOIS, IS A SUBURB LOCATED forty miles northwest of Chicago. It is a largely homogenous community of just over twenty thousand residents. To an outsider, little differentiates this middle-to-upper-class suburb from thousands of others located near major American cities. The town's most famous resident was the Oscar-winning actor Marlon Brando, who attended (though he never finished) Libertyville High School in the late 1930s. Moreover, there have been other Libertyville products of note: two major league baseball players, Brett Butler and Cy Young award–winning pitcher Mike Marshall, grew up in Libertyville; additionally, twice-defeated presidential candidate Governor Adlai Stevenson called his farm in Libertyville home for more than thirty years. Otherwise, the town has enjoyed relative anonymity since its incorporation as the village of Libertyville back in 1882.

During the spring of 2006, the mayor of Libertyville, Jeffrey Harger, began to trumpet the town's recently adopted slogan: "Libertyville—the spirit of independence." To Harger, "these four words describe the philosophy and heritage of our village."[1] Yet, some students attending the town's high school may be forgiven if they believe otherwise. That past February, school officials of Community School District 128 (which contains Libertyville and one other town) decided to inject the town's high school into the growing national debate over how to treat the latest Internet fad: students' social-networking websites such as MySpace.com and Facebook.com. The school board declared that all "illegal" or "inappropriate" behavior on such sites would thereafter serve as a cause for disciplinary action, if not outright expulsion. None of the board members were at all deterred by the fact that Libertyville High School maintained no formal arrangement with either of the two websites, and thus arguably had no jurisdiction over students' posting material on those websites from home or during nonschool hours.

What spurred officials at Community School District 128 to regulate students' online activities so aggressively? In recent years, these social-networking websites have become venues for abusive behavior among teenagers at high schools, middle schools, and even some elementary schools. Websites like MySpace.com routinely feature publicly accessible postings that include obscene and profane language directed at others, sometimes referred to as "cyberbullying." Some students' willingness to post photographs online has also given pause to school officials in District 128, as well as elsewhere. In one highly publicized instance at a middle school, a group of girls posed in their underwear for pictures that were eventually made available on a social-networking site.[2] Photographs of students engaging in drug use or alcohol consumption have spurred other principals into action as well.

The reaction of school officials to some of the activities described above is easy to explain: drug and alcohol use, certain types of harassment, and what may arguably be considered a form of child pornography are all illegal activities, and schools may be liable in a different way if they discover evidence of those activities and take no action to stop them. Still, schools are normally not held liable for incidents that occur off campus and during nonschool hours, especially when those incidents are wholly unrelated to any school-sponsored activities. Unfortunately, activities that occur on the Internet are not so easy to categorize. Most schools maintain computers where students may post or read the offensive material, even if it is privately sent. The proliferation of handheld devices that send e-mails or surf the Web, devices such as BlackBerries, iPods, or even simple cellular phones, allows students to engage in online activities while on campus during normal school hours. Even more significantly, even when online activity originates outside of the physical school building, some courts have held schools responsible for the intentional acts of another student, so long as those acts could reasonably have been anticipated.[3] Given these facts and the ever-present threat of lawsuits charging negligence or inaction, few principals and school boards are in a position to offhandedly dismiss illegal activities or harassment posted on the Internet as lying outside their legitimate authority.

Far more controversial, however, have been school authorities' various attempts to supervise (and if necessary, punish) online activities that are either offensive or (in the words of the District 128 policy) "inappropriate" but may still be legal. One of the core purposes of websites such as Facebook.com and MySpace.com is to provide a forum for students to speak out and express their opinions to friends, acquaintances, and others on a range of issues. Sometimes those issues are personal (e.g., the desire to find a suitable romantic companion, the desire to get tickets to a sold-out concert); at other times, they concern public issues (e.g., opinions on abortion or religion, criticism of elected officials, and even criticism of school officials). By the latter half of 2006, social-networking websites had established themselves as an extremely popular means for students to communicate with each other, competing with cell phone conversations, cell phone text messaging, and even more traditional e-mailing through a server such as AOL or Yahoo!.

This much is clear: school officials around the country are entering uncharted territory when it comes to overseeing student publications on the Internet. Can they regulate such speech, and if so, how? Consider the following episodes that recently received considerable national attention:

- In New Jersey, the Oceanport School District spent $117,500 in a settlement agreement after a student was suspended for putting up a website from home that harshly criticized his middle school and compared the school's principal to a dictator.[4]
- In St. Louis, Missouri, a Kirkwood High School student, along with some of his classmates, posted from the computer in his house a "hot "or "not hot" list of one hundred junior high school girls on Facebook.com; the list included some lewd descriptions of the girls' bodies. Although the list was never physically brought to school, five boys received ten-day suspensions for participating in the venture. "These remarks were personal and cruel," said school district spokeswoman Nona King in defense of the school's actions.[5]
- In San Diego, California, a female Del Mar Heights Elementary School student created a page on MySpace.com that included references to romantic incidents among students during recess and made some disparaging remarks about her own relationships with boys at the school. The principal of the school, Wendy Wardlow, responded by asking "every parent to sign an agreement that included a commitment to monitor their children's computer use at home to prevent 'cyberbullying', on-line gossip and the use of obscene and profane language." "I probably overstepped my bounds," Wardlow admitted later.[6]
- In Longview, Washington, school officials banned MySpace.com from all school computers because of "inappropriate or possible inappropriate content," such as uncensored photographs, comments, and "pretty much unrestricted dialogue."[7]

Unlike MySpace.com, Facebook.com has gained popularity on college campuses in particular; as of early December 2007, the website had the largest number of registered users among college-focused sites, with fifty-seven million active members worldwide. Thus, college administrators as well have been forced to take notice of these websites. Naturally, students who are still minors attending high school, middle school, and elementary school introduce a far thornier set of factors into the mix. On one hand, school officials have extra responsibilities for supervising minors under their care than do college administrators overseeing the activities of those who are over eighteen years old. At the same time, most teenagers live at home, where their online actions are difficult, if not impossible, to monitor. That has not stopped some principals from trying, as the episodes listed above make clear.

The questions raised by this new medium are significant. What are school officials' powers under such circumstances? Is the regulation by authorities of student opinions in general, and student online expression in particular, consistent with the First Amendment? The answers to these questions may well depend on how one characterizes the medium of social-networking sites, the school itself, and the means by which the schools attempt to regulate such expression.

Discussion of the issues surrounding the regulation of social-networking sites sets the stage for a broader discussion of the state of free expression in the nation's high schools. Students posting news and information on social-networking sites are not just acting as reporters: they are their own editors and self-publishers. Principals are not in a position to censor students' expression prior to its publication on the Internet (although they may try to punish students for material they have posted after the fact). Essentially, the First Amendment no longer frames prior negotiations between students, their teachers, and the principals; students apply these First Amendment freedoms on their own. How, if at all, does this new paradigm for student media affect the perceptions students have of the First Amendment and free expression? In particular, do students who post material on websites like MySpace.com and others hold fundamentally different attitudes about their freedoms than students who do not blog or use such sites? How do their attitudes compare with the attitudes of (1) students who take classes in the media and the First Amendment, and (2) students who participate in more "traditional" forms of media, such as student newspapers, magazines, TV stations, and radio stations? Given the realities of this new media age, is civic education even capable of training students to understand and appreciate free press rights?

The Digital Generation

The definition of "digital media," or "new media," is a subject of some scholarly debate, and a comprehensive review of that debate would go well beyond the purview of this book.[9] Still, some introduction to these terms is warranted. In *The Language of New Media*,[10] Lev Manovich argues that the term "new media" began to appear in the press for the first time in the literature in 1990 and encompasses any and all new cultural forms that depend on computers for presentation and distribution, including websites, virtual worlds, virtual reality, multimedia, computer games, and computer animation. In short, Manovich believes "new media" is a form of shorthand for the computerization of the culture. "Digital media" invokes a similar concept.

Whether or not one accepts Manovich's definition, the current generation of teens takes for granted all these forms of media in a way that no adult over the age of thirty-five may fully comprehend, save perhaps the parents of teens or others who are exposed to students and their technology on a daily basis. For purposes of the analysis that follows, we define the "new media," or "digital media," as media forms that allow their users to freely disseminate materials at their discretion. These media forms provide a means of communications that utilize either or both of the following:

- the relative novelty of digital computing
- the unprecedented speed of the evolution and mutation of devices and technologies

Different generations may actually perceive old media types in different ways precisely because digital media often gives way to old media slowly and without much fanfare. For example, older generations may view still photography as a product of cameras and cameralike devices that "write on" or "record on" a physical medium such as plastic tape. By contrast, the current generation views still photography as just another aspect of "digital reproduction" that takes up space on a hard drive; beyond that, it enjoys no physical manifestation whatsoever unless and until someone decides to print out the picture on a printer.

The term "digital media" does not just invoke images of increased convenience for those willing to learn and understand how these technologies work (although that may be one result). Nor does it merely entail decreasing the costs of communication (another inevitable consequence, though usually only after an outlay of significantly greater costs at the beginning). Rather, it has become a source of identity for the current younger generation of Americans.

How these media manifest themselves among high school students is this book's principle area of concern. Consider the following aspects of the new media that form distinctive elements of this modern youth culture:

1. **Portable computing:** High school students now equipped with their own laptops or personal digital assistants can do word processing and

play games literally anywhere; they are no longer anchored to their desks or even to places where electrical outlets are readily available.

2. **The Internet as a source of news and information:** Computers are not just portable, but through the Internet, they offer a virtually unlimited store of knowledge organized and interpreted by others. Nearly every well-known newspaper or magazine around the world sponsors its own website on the Internet. And while its accuracy may be questioned, the Internet encyclopedia *Wikipedia* offers students over two million articles with links to other websites. Students today thus take for granted that they have a readily available "library" open to them at any time of the day with a mere push of a button. Meanwhile, physical libraries remain important not just as places that contain actual books and periodicals but also as locations where Internet access is available and subscription databases may be accessed and searched.

3. **Digital entertainment:** So-called digital technology refers to the conversion of real-world information currently stored on fixed objects (records, tapes, etc.) to data-carrying signals that may be stored on a variety of devices or databases. Once this information is in digital form, it becomes possible to make multiple-generation copies that are identical to the original; moreover, hardware is able to amplify the digital signal and pass it on with no loss of information. Students thus enjoy access to immense amounts of entertainment, such as music, video, audiobooks, and the like, through relatively small and portable digital playing devices.

4. **E-mail and the use of the Internet for two-way communications:** Because the Internet is a two-way, interactive medium, it also serves as an alternative means of communicating with friends, family members, and even complete strangers through e-mail. Chat groups and discussion lists form around topics of interest as literal communities of people are formed on the Internet.

5. **The Internet as a means of personal publication:** Millions of teenagers around the country now routinely post information and thoughts on their own websites, which are then made available to members of the same social-networking site or to the public at large. Social-networking sites such as MySpace.com and Facebook.com allow users to post text, pictures, videos, and links to almost anywhere else on the Internet.

Concerns about the digital media have focused primarily on the loss of privacy they encourage. The ability to store and use large amounts of diverse information makes it possible to track individual activities and interests to an unprecedented degree. Indeed, some critics complain that virtually every aspect of modern life has been captured and stored in some digital form. When an individual shops today at a large grocery store or drug store in the United States, he or she must be willing to trade personal information for a discount on groceries or other products. The stores carefully collect information about each member's buying habits, not only to improve ways of doing business in general but to target individual customers with discounts and other offers based on the preferences they have exhibited. In the digital age, everyone loses some degree of the anonymity that was once intrinsic to our understanding of privacy.[11] It also eases the path for criminals to engage in identity theft, acquiring or using another person's personal data for their own illicit financial gain.

Meanwhile, comparatively less attention has been paid to the implications the digital media revolution has for democracy and the way that students, parents, teachers, and school officials alike come to view rights central to democracy, such as the freedoms of speech and of the press. The proliferation of computers with Internet access in every school and library throughout the nation has eased the fears of a growing "digital divide" in which lower socioeconomic classes would have limited Internet access and all the benefits it offers. In fact, the Internet today is a more democratic medium than most others, with 97 percent of high school students in 2006 reporting they had Internet access at school, and 87 percent saying they had Internet access at home. (See figure 4.1)

The shrinking price of desktop computers has also contributed to this democratizing trend. Moreover, the ability to share information so easily and rapidly on a global scale has brought with it a heightened level of free expres-

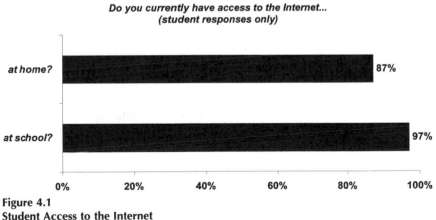

Figure 4.1
Student Access to the Internet
Source: FOFA 2006

sion for those who post materials on the Internet. Individuals and organizations suddenly have the ability to publish on any topic to a global audience at a negligible cost, particularly in comparison to any previous communication technology.

"Blogging," "Posting," and the Freedom of the Press

Of course, the central question that principals (and eventually courts) must grapple with concerns the degree to which First Amendment protection applies to student blogs, e-mails, and other communications posted on social-networking sites and elsewhere. Because First Amendment protection in this context depends on the nature of the student publication, including how it has traditionally been treated by students and school officials, some background description of Web publications, major social-networking sites, and their implications for our understanding of the press is first necessary.

The dominance of the Internet as a means of communication both in the United States and globally is no longer subject to debate. According to Internet World statistics published online as of May 15, 2007, over 1.1 billion people around the world currently use the Internet, including 400 million users in Asia alone.[12] The Internet is the principal means by which individuals outside of the same internal network can send electronic messages (e-mail) to each other without incurring paper costs or significant transportation and shipping costs. At least twelve billion pages make up the World Wide Web, a global read-write information space of immense size and impact.

One of the most significant benefits of the Internet is that it empowers anybody with a computer and Internet access to disseminate information to millions of people in an instant. Some scholars refer to this development as the Internet's "democratizing influence" on the media, as the cost of contributing news, information, and opinions into the marketplace of ideas via the Internet has become increasingly negligible. Perhaps the first manifestation of this development, one that put all the more mainstream outlets on notice of the changes taking place in this medium, emerged in the form of the *Drudge Report*, an online newsletter generated by Matt Drudge from his desktop computer at home beginning in the early 1990s. A former manager of the CBS Studios gift shop in Hollywood, California, Drudge packed his column with news and gossip about Hollywood. He originally distributed the news by e-mail, but then, beginning in 1996, Drudge transitioned the newsletter over to his own site on the World Wide Web. Drudge also shifted his emphasis from Hollywood gossip to political gossip, and his timing could not have been any more fortuitous. Drudge is credited both with breaking the news that Republican presidential candidate Bob Dole had chosen Jack Kemp as his running mate in 1996 and with helping to break the Bill Clinton–Monica Lewinsky scandal in 1998. By 2003, Drudge's website was taking in $3,500 a day in advertising revenues, a product of the millions of page views he receives every day.[13]

University of Tennessee professor Glenn Reynolds writes in *An Army of Davids: How Markets and Technology Empower Ordinary People to Beat Big Media, Big Government and Other Goliaths* that the Internet in effect broke the long-standing chokehold on public information and discussion that the mainstream media had traditionally maintained.[14] All these outlets have rushed to get their own websites up and running in response to these rapid developments, and nearly all offer free access to the public, granted generally after the prospective reader has registered with the website, a process that takes less than a minute in most cases.[15]

What are the implications of this democratization of the news media on the quality of news and information? Certainly, quality is not a given even among the mainstream news media. In 2003 it was discovered that Jayson Blair, a *New York Times* reporter, had repeatedly committed journalistic fraud by manufacturing quotes for stories and plagiarizing from other newspapers.[16] On September 20, 2004, CBS News was forced to retract a story that its news anchor, Dan Rather, had reported two weeks earlier concerning President George W. Bush's National Guard service. Relying on documents found in the personal files of a military officer, Rather had reported that Bush had been found unfit for flying status; in fact, the documents' authenticity was brought quickly into question, as many of the experts cited by CBS began to contradict the story. The Blair and Rather affairs lend credence to claims by Reynolds and others that millions of Americans who were once in awe of the "punditocracy" of major networks and newspapers now realize that "many unknowns can do it better than the lords of the profession."[17] All this contributes to the premise that Internet journalism has led to a "journalism without journalists" in which private individuals conducting "citizen journalism" have supplanted traditional news organizations, transforming the nature of the media in the process.[18]

Further complicating this new and changing tableau of the "press" has been the increasing popularity of blogging. Short for "weblogs," blogs are essentially websites where entries are made as in a journal or diary, but in reverse chronological order. According to a June 2006 study conducted by the Pew Internet & American Life Project, twelve million Americans currently maintain blogs, while fifty-seven million Americans profess to reading blogs.[19] Are these "bloggers" members of the press? Whether or not traditional mainstream news outlets think so may be irrelevant: fully 34 percent of the bloggers consider what they do a form of journalism—that's four million members of the press who may wish to seek press credentials in the not-so-distant future. Moreover, many of these bloggers report spending extra time verifying facts included in a posting to their blog and include links to original source material that has been cited or in some way used in a post. Indeed, more than a third of bloggers (35 percent) say they have performed both of these two activities often.[20]

Mainstream news outlets might also be having difficulty dismissing all these new bloggers from their profession because they are increasingly credited with uncovering facts that more traditional news organizations have not discovered. To be sure, there's power in numbers; it's hard to compete with four million private reporters scattered all over the nation and the globe. Whereas network newscasts and national newspapers are understandably reluctant to tell stories that will upset important people absent mounds of evidence, most bloggers are more willing to make sensationalistic claims. And if those claims are later verified, the mainstream news outlets may be able to claim journalistic responsibility, but the bloggers will get the credit for being there first. In Rather's case, the authenticity of documents the anchorman cited was quickly called into question by conservative and liberal bloggers alike.

The developments listed above have had a significant influence on the press in general and on the manner in which it does business. It was only a matter of time before students in the nation's public schools fell in line with these trends as well. School districts working with tightened budgets have led the way in encouraging low-cost Internet publications as part of journalism-education programs, often at the expense of creating new student publication outlets such as student newspapers, magazines, radio stations, and television stations. Based on percentages drawn from the John S. and James L. Knight Foundation's 2004 Future of the First Amendment (FOFA) survey, between 1999 and 2004, while an average of 570 student newspapers were created per year, 424 student newspapers were eliminated on average over the same period. Meanwhile, more student magazines, radio stations, and television stations were eliminated on average during the same period. The most marked contrast comes with Internet publications: nearly five hundred sixty-seven student Internet publications were created per year over that five-year period, as compared to less than one hundred eliminated. Thus, as table 4.1 makes clear, the creation of student Internet media is clearly driving the trend toward more media activity in general.

Of course, these figures only account for formal Internet publications officially created and sanctioned by school officials. Many of these publications play a critical role in journalism-education programs and are considered an essential part of any strong journalism curriculum. Teacher advisors often play a role here as well: in the 2004 survey, 13 percent of the nation's high

Table 4.1
Student Media Outlets Created/Eliminated, 1999–2004
(Based on Population of 20,375 Schools Nationwide)

	Created (per-year average)	Eliminated (per-year average)
Newspapers	570	424
Magazines	78	114
Radio stations	37	79
TV stations	228	245
Internet publications	567	96
Total	**1,480**	**958**

Source: FOFA 2004 survey of school administrators.

school teachers reported serving as a faculty advisor for one or more of the various student publications or news outlets at their respective schools.

Lost in the shuffle has been the growth of student publications, usually Internet publications, that play an important role in communicating news and information to students but do not serve any formal role within the curriculum. Underground student publications have long played an important role in publicizing events and information; the Internet age now provides students with a nearly unlimited amount of space to transmit information about news and events at a particular time—and to transmit it widely.

This sets the stage for social-networking sites that serve as portals for a plethora of student functions. A student's Web page (usually pages) may feature blogs, user profiles, groups, photos, and an Internet e-mail system—a sort of "one website fits all." Given their immense popularity at schools across the country, some of the most popular social-networking sites require some more detailed explanation.

MySpace.com: The most popular social-networking site on the Web, MySpace.com boasted more than one hundred million registered accounts as of August 2006; the company estimates that 25 percent of its users are teenagers.[21] No greater vote of endorsement exists than that cast by Rupert Murdoch's News Corp, which bought MySpace for $580 million in July 2005. Of course, the name of the game is growth: traffic on MySpace grew by 318 percent in 2005 alone. Additionally, the traffic on social-networking sites tends to be intense rather than casual: students who come to the website usually "hang out" there for quite a while. Many students spend two hours per day on the website, if not more, which amounts to a dream come true for advertisers who buy their way onto this free, ad-supported networking site.[22]

What makes MySpace.com so attractive to teenagers? Students who visit the website start by registering and setting up their profile. Each profile contains

two standard blurbs: (1) "About me," and (2) "Who I'd like to meet." Standard profiles include information about the user's likes and dislikes in movies, television, music, and the like and allow users to upload pictures, videos, or anything else. The profile may also contain a blog. Each user can select a designated number of people for the "top friends" area. Student users are free to choose any community they wish to participate in from different high schools or even from colleges and universities. The registered user can also customize his or her site to block certain people from visiting. Frequent MySpace users redecorate their pages, put up their own art or photographs, write poetry, play music for friends, and anything else one might imagine.

Critics of MySpace complain that the distance afforded by the Internet emboldens individuals to publish controversial photos or to make controversial statements that they would not make in person or in more well-established media. In essence, the rebellious nature of the medium encourages compromising photos, gossip, and malicious comments. At least one college, Del Mar Community College, blocked all on-campus access to MySpace in early 2006 on the grounds that network strain from excessive MySpace traffic was consuming too much of the college's bandwidth, impeding the college's own Web-based courses. Whether a college or high school could take the same action solely because of objections to content remains to be seen.

Facebook.com: Though much smaller than MySpace.com (over twenty-five million members registered in February 2007), Facebook.com maintains the largest number of registered users among sites that focus on college-student accounts in particular. Though the vast majority of its users are college students, anyone with access to a valid e-mail address from one of more than two thousand universities and colleges can register for the site, including alumni, faculty, and staff.

Facebook's focus on the college market has not led to the exclusion of high school students from the site. Recognizing this reality, on February 27, 2006, the site effectively integrated the high school and college levels of the site; users from the two different branches can now interact so long as they are already established as friends. Many college users complained bitterly about the decision to integrate, fearing that the website would now be susceptible to many of the same problems experienced on MySpace, including excessive spammers, stalkers, or worse.

As with MySpace, some colleges and universities have tried to block access to Facebook on their campuses. Most notably, the University of New Mexico (UNM) in October 2005 blocked access to the website "on campus computers and networks" on the grounds that unsolicited e-mails and an imposter website (UNM Facebook) were transmitting erroneous information to members of the UNM community. Meanwhile, many high schools across the United States have

banned Facebook.com on all of its school computers, a concededly limited action in response to antischool groups have had proliferated on Facebook.

All these websites pose a significant threat to the freedom of the press students currently enjoy. Because social-networking sites in particular are so susceptible to abuse, often acting as the transmission device for various forms of harassment, slander, and inappropriate images, school officials are eager to regulate such sites. High school and middle school officials in particular cite *Reno v. ACLU*,[23] *New York v. Ferber*,[24] and other Supreme Court precedents that allow the government to regulate websites and video imagery involving minors more aggressively than would be allowed for adults. Yet, in *Reno v. ACLU*, the Supreme Court struck down the federal Internet indecency law because of incidental harms it caused to constitutionally protected speech; the same risk is run when school officials censor social-networking sites. More significantly, the websites themselves are in cyberspace, thus accessible to students in many places outside of school officials' direct control.

What does such censorship imply for student perceptions of free expression rights? As was noted above, blogs and networking sites turn every student immediately into a reporter/publisher from the moment he or she goes online. If students can legitimately be grouped in with professional news journalists and members of the so-called mainstream media, school censorship of their activities serves to dilute the freedom of the press both in theory and in practice. As will be seen in the next chapter, the new learning paradigm of students as publishers creates a powerful tool in the framework of civics education. But it also carries with it significant responsibilities—for parents, the school officials, and the students themselves.

"Digital Media"–Savvy Parents and the General Population

In *The Perfect Thing: How the iPod Shuffles Commerce, Culture, and Coolness*, author Steven Levy offers a paean to "the most familiar, and certainly the most desirable, new object of the twenty-first century."[25] For the current generation of Millennials, iPods and other cutting-edge forms of technology don't just facilitate communications; among teenagers in particular, such devices help them to make a fashion statement. iPods, cell phones, portable gaming devices, and other devices today come in all shapes, colors, and styles. On a visit to many of the nation's high schools, one may see this technology on display everywhere: in the classroom, in the lunchroom, and in the hallways.

Of course, iPods are not the only devices of choice for today's generation of teenagers. Laptop computers, handheld organizers such as BlackBerries, and even cell phones appear everywhere. At home, the personal computer has become a staple of the average American household. Still, a central question remains: is this new, technologically sophisticated online culture transforming the way students view information dissemination, journalists, and the constitutional rights that traditionally protect them? Even more significantly, as student use of MySpace.com and Facebook.com has become so widespread, does student participation as journalists or bloggers in these digital media affect the way they view the media, whether new or old?

In late 2004, the Pew Internet & American Life Project surveyed parents (with and without online teens) on their use of new media.[26] The parents' extensive use of new media may actually surprise some: 87 percent of the parents of online teens say they access the Internet or World Wide Web to send and receive e-mail. Of those parents of online teens who do go online themselves, 20 percent say they use a wireless device like a personal digital assistant (PDA), cell phone, or wireless laptop, and more than half (55 percent) say they feel that e-mail and the Internet have been a good thing for their children.

What about "blogging" and other journalistic applications of the new media? A subsequent Pew survey in January 2005 took up this subject, discovering that even as the use of blogs has exploded, the phenomenon has still been limited mostly to a minority of the overall population. Surveying the general adult population, the Pew study found that blog readership shot up by 58 percent during the course of 2004 to an overall readership of thirty-two million Americans. In all, 27 percent of adult Internet users said they read blogs at the time of the survey. Moreover, just under one in ten Internet users indicated that they regularly or sometimes read political blogs during the 2004 election campaign.[27]

Even more significant are the numbers of individuals who say they actually create and post on blogs. The Pew Internet & American Life Project began asking about blog creation in the spring of 2002. At that time, 3 percent of Internet users said they had created a blog or Web diary; two years later, the figure grew to 5 percent, and by late 2004, the number had grown to 7 percent. Who are blog creators? According to the Pew survey, they tend to be more male (57 percent) and young (48 percent are under thirty).

Profiling New Media Usage among High School Students

The Knight Foundation's 2004 and 2006 FOFA surveys sought to investigate digital media trends and the role these media play in socializing high school students in particular. Clearly, the digital divide has shrunk to a degree. In

2006, 87 percent of high school students said they had access to the Internet at home, and 97 percent said they had access at school. Even the vast majority of lower-income students have access to the Internet at school: 89 percent of that group said they enjoyed such access in 2006. So, how are students using the Internet, and what role does it play, if any, in civic education?

Student Access to New Media for News and Information

Online or Internet news sources have proliferated during recent years, but that does not mean they have replaced television news and newspapers entirely. As figure 4.2 indicates, in 2006 a little more than half (51 percent) of students said they got news and information from online sources at least once per week.

Figure 4.3 shows that those students who said they went online for news at least occasionally, by far the greatest percentage (66 percent) said they used the news pages of Internet source providers such as Google News, Yahoo! News, and the like at least once per week. Significantly lower percentages said they looked directly at network TV news websites (45 percent), the websites of major national newspapers (21 percent), or the websites of local newspapers or TV

How often, if at all, do you get news and information from online or Internet sources in general? (Student respondents only)

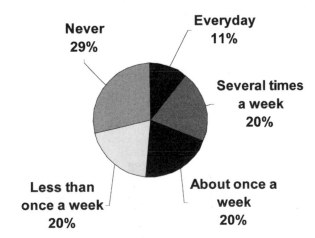

Figure 4.2
Student Reliance on the Internet for News—2006

stations (34 percent) at least once per week. Of course, given that Google News, Yahoo! News, and other Internet source providers simply act as a conduit, sending the user to sources such as nytimes.com for news, these figures may be misleading. Students know how they get on to the Internet to launch their search for news, but they may be far less aware of where they land.

Blogging offers a different and more personal news source for consumers of news. Some blogs are extremely well-known and widely visited, such as the *Huffington Post* (political commentator Ariana Huffington's blog, linked to by over fourteen thousand other blogs) and the writer Andrew Sullivan's blog, *The Daily Dish*. Yet, the vast majority of blogs are written by relatively unknown figures or by individuals known primarily within a limited circle of specialists or experts. Additionally, social-networking sites such as MySpace .com and Facebook.com offer all users the chance to disseminate blogs to millions of others, and many of them do exactly that.

Almost half (48 percent) of the students in the Knight survey in 2006 said they used blogs to get news and information, with almost a third (32 percent) indicating that they accessed blogs for news at least once per week. Interestingly, female students (36 percent) were more likely than male students (28 percent) to get news and information from blogs at least once a week. Although the digital divide among socioeconomic classes had lessened considerably, some division did remain in this context: while 17 percent of those students identifying themselves as rich said they got news and information from blogs every day, just 7 percent of lower-income students and 11 percent of poor students said they did so.

High school students offer their own unique ranking of the quality of news sources as well. Of all the various media sources, 45 percent of the high school students surveyed rank television as the best overall source of news, 44 percent say television stations are the most accurate source of news, and

Percentage of student online users who say they use each of the following at least once a week to get news and information:

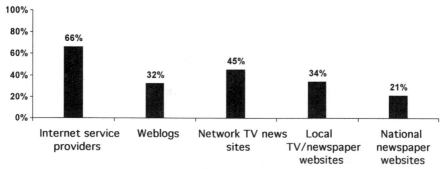

Figure 4.3
Student Reliance on Different Sources for News—2006
Source: FOFA 2006

43 percent say they consider the television stations the easiest news source to use. And in fact, no other news source rates close to television on these various measures. Just 23 percent say newspapers are the best overall source of news, ranking second to television. And, as figure 4.4 indicates, 35 percent say newspapers are the most accurate, and Internet publications other than blogs finishes second among high school students for being the easiest source of news to use.

Old Media versus Digital Media: Comparing High School Students and Teachers

A generation gap between teachers and their students is especially evident in this context. Not surprisingly, faculty members are more loyal to old media news sources than the current generation of high school students. In FOFA 2004, 55 percent of the teachers said they got news from newspapers every day (91 percent said they read newspapers at least once a week). By contrast, just 13 percent of students said they got news from newspapers daily, with 18 percent of high school students admitting that they *never* got information from newspapers. Local television newscasts garnered daily attention from 63 percent of teachers, while just 41 percent of high school students received information from television as a whole, national or local.

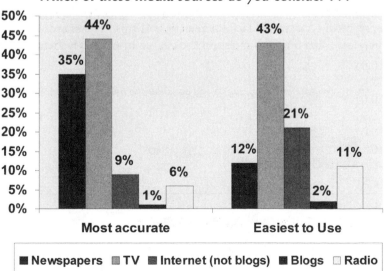

Figure 4.4
Student Perceptions of News Media Accuracy and Ease of Use—2006
Source: FOFA 2006

Compare those old media habits to those that have arisen with regard to digital media. When faculty members were asked in 2004 how often they got news from the Internet, just 32 percent said they used the Internet every day for those purposes. Meanwhile, 21 percent of the teachers said they *never* used the Internet to gather news and information. By contrast, in 2004, one in five students said they got news from the Internet every day, and 58 percent said they got news from that source at least once per week.

How do teachers rate these digital media sources? Unlike their students, teachers in 2006 were also far more likely to favor newspapers over other media forms as the best overall source of news (48 percent). Among the faculty members surveyed, television stations lagged in second place, far behind at 28 percent. Interestingly, the digital gap appears to work the other way in this context: while just 10 percent of high school students ranked Internet publications as the best overall source of news, 15 percent of faculty members did so. That may be a product of what type of Internet publications the two different groups rely on. While students were more apt to get their news from blogs found on MySpace.com (32 percent said they did so at least once per week), teachers more frequently turned to websites of major national newspapers and were less likely to rely on blogs. Indeed, a mere 7 percent of teachers reported looking at online journals such as blogs at least once per week.

The above difference has significant implications for the way journalism is taught in the schools. Given that 72 percent of the teachers surveyed said they had *never* received news and information from blogs, it is highly unlikely that they would come to view blogs as something to be covered in standard journalism or media courses. In fact, the rejection of this news source by teachers is so pervasive that one may question the degree to which teachers even view

Which of these media sources do you consider the best overall source of news?

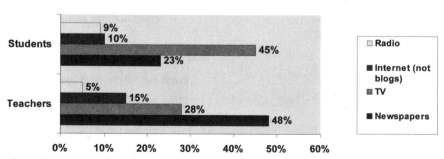

Figure 4.5
Student Views on News Media as the "Best Overall Source of News"—2006
Source: FOFA 2006

blogs and online diaries as a legitimate form of journalism. And given that almost half (48 percent) admitted to getting news and information from blogs at least some of the time, are students likely to take seriously a journalism class that refuses to take that news source seriously?

Student Exercise of Free Press Rights Using Digital Media Outlets

Just as importantly, not only do students today access digital media sources for news and information, but they actively participate in news dissemination as online reporters, editors, and publishers. Blogging is just one manifestation of the new media, which empowers students to exercise freedom of speech and the press without the economic constraints traditionally imposed on writers and speakers in the past, who needed expensive television time or access to a printing press to get their message across to the masses.

Adhering to patterns in the general adult population reported by Pew and others, in 2006 many high school students reported using the Internet to communicate with others through e-mail, online discussions, and weblogs. Specifically, 71 percent of American high school students reported sending and receiving e-mails at least once a week (30 percent said they e-mailed every day). Females are apparently more frequent users of e-mail: 34 percent of the high school girls surveyed said they sent or received e-mails every day, as compared to just 25 percent of male high school students who said they did so. Additionally, 44 percent of the high school students surveyed participated in online discussions, chat groups, or both at least once a week (18 percent did so every day). In this case, the gender gap is not so pronounced (19 percent of girls said they participated every day, as compared to 17 percent of boys).

Meanwhile, the posting of messages and information in the form of weblogs, whether on social-networking sites or elsewhere, has exploded in recent years. Has this trickled down into the high schools as well? As indicated in figure 4.6, 32 percent of the students surveyed in 2006 reported posting messages or opinions to online columns (i.e., weblogs) at least weekly, with one in ten students reporting that they did so every day. In all, nearly half the high school population (44 percent) reported posting messages or opinions to online columns or diaries at some point during the past year.

Who are the primary bloggers in the nation's high schools? Certainly, it pays to have extra leisure time to engage in these activities: according to FOFA 2006, one in five students who identified themselves as "rich" said they posted messages or opinions to online columns or blogs on a daily basis. By comparison, just 12 percent of those who described their families as "upper-income" reported daily blogging, and no more than 10 percent of any other economic strata indicated that they did so. In all, 46 percent of the high-income students said they blogged at least once a week, as compared to just 29 percent and 32 percent of the middle-income and poor high school students, respectively.

In contrast to the large gender gap indicated by high school students who e-mail, females in high school (11 percent) were only slightly more likely than male students (9 percent) to be daily bloggers; that gap increases somewhat when examining those who blog at least weekly (34 percent of the female students said they did, as compared to 29 percent of males). And apparently there is no racial gap when it comes to blogging, as 30 percent of black students and 31 percent of white students reported that they blogged at least once per week (35 percent of Hispanic high school students reported blogging at least once per week, marking a higher rate than either of the other two groups).

Teaching with Digital Media: A View from the Classroom

A clear generation gap between teachers and students was already revealed earlier in this chapter: students access blogs and online diaries for news and information far more often than their own teachers report doing so. Teachers may be acting in this regard based on their own reasonable perceptions that news and information transmitted in this form is inherently less reliable: bloggers need not be well educated or experienced journalists; many just offer ran-

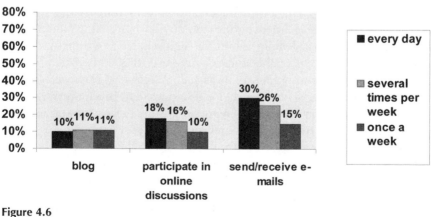

How often, if at all, do you use the Internet, the World Wide Web or an online service to...

Figure 4.6
Student Participation on the Internet—2006
Source: FOFA 2006

dom thoughts on events that may not even qualify as "hard news" in any real sense. Still, an effective educational process requires that teachers address and react to this gap. Teachers express a theoretical desire to train students in the ways of digital media literacy. Fully 85 percent of those surveyed said that they felt it was *very* important that all students learn to use the Internet or World Wide Web effectively to collect news and information, and just 1 percent dismissed this medium as either not too important or not important at all. But is there any evidence that these opinions are translating into the curriculum?

In truth, there is mixed evidence on this score. Recall that 55 percent of the nation's high school teachers indicated that they required as an assignment that their students either read a newspaper or watch television, and 28 percent of teachers required that students do so on no less than a monthly basis. Apparently, teachers have not shied away from requiring Internet research as well: fully 86 percent said they had required as part of an assignment that students do research using the World Wide Web or Internet. Moreover, 38 percent required assignments such as these on at least a monthly basis, and 12 percent required that their students do online research *on a weekly basis*. Clearly, the nation's teachers have bought into the premise that research no longer takes place just in traditional, book-filled libraries.

On the other hand, while faculty members' willingness to incorporate Internet research into assignments is one thing, their willingness to utilize the Internet as a means of communications within the classroom is another thing entirely: 86 percent of teachers reported that they had never required as part of an assignment that students communicate with each other by e-mail, chat group, or some other form of online discussion. And of the remaining 14 percent who had utilized the Internet in that fashion, half required it no more often than a few times per year.

Entertainment Programming: The Final Piece of the New Media Puzzle

We have already established that the current generation of high school students relies on many traditional news sources for news and information. At the same time, they have also been the driving force behind the proliferation of blogs and online diaries, both as consumers and journalists.

And yet, something is still missing from the profile of students that has been generated so far. To be sure, no one news source has managed to capture an overwhelming percentage of the high school students' market. But there are some names that grab a significant majority of students' attention, as evidenced by the large crowds that convene whenever they appear on college campuses. The reference here is to such entertainers as Jon Stewart and Steven Colbert, who satirize news stories and events daily on the *Daily Show* and *Colbert Report*, respectively. This also refers to shows like *South Park* and *Saturday Night Live,* which poke fun at politicians and news events on a regular basis.

Just how influential are such entertainment programs? According to figure 4.7 drawn from FOFA 2006, fully 46 percent of the high school students surveyed said they got news and information at least once a week from entertainment programs that discuss current events, such as the *Daily Show,* the *Colbert Report,* and *South Park.* And, in fact, fully two-thirds (67 percent) admitted to getting news and information from those shows at least occasionally. These numbers exclude students who watched those shows purely for entertainment, as opposed to for news and information. Interestingly, high school students seem aware of the limits to this type of news source: just 7 percent ranked these shows as the best overall news source available, and a mere 3 percent considered them the most accurate way of learning news and information. But their high visibility among high school students makes them a force in the modern age of media.

Which groups are most likely to rely on the *Daily Show,* the *Colbert Report,* and *South Park* for news and information? Certainly, male high school students are far more attracted to this medium than females. Three in four male students reported using this medium to gather news, with 12 percent saying they watched the shows *every day.* By comparison, just 59 percent of females used the medium, with only 4 percent using it every day. Among those who gathered news from these shows every day, there was no difference at all between African American students (8 percent) and white students. Meanwhile,

How often, if at all, do you get news and information from entertainment programs that feature some discussion of current events such as The Daily Show, The Colbert Report, and South Park? (Student respondents only)

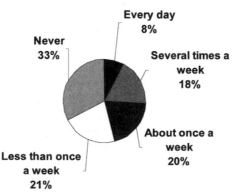

Figure 4.7
Student Reliance on Entertainment Programs for News—2006

students who identified themselves as rich were the subgroup most likely to watch those types of shows every day (17 percent report doing so).

Again, it may seem surprising to some that while males and students from wealthy families tend to rely on these shows more often, that does not necessarily translate into confidence in the medium's accuracy and validity. Just 8 percent of male students and students from wealthy families felt that such entertainment shows were the best overall source of news, a mere one-point increase over the percentage of high school students overall who felt that way (just 7 percent). Similarly, just 3 percent of males *and* females rated these entertainment shows the most accurate news source. What's the bottom line? While certain groups prefer these shows more than other groups, everyone seems aware that what they are getting is, after all, intended as a form of entertainment.

As a final means of putting these entertainment shows into proper perspective, FOFA 2006 also surveyed teachers about news sources in general. Among high school teachers, barely 1 percent rated entertainment programs featuring current events as the best overall source of news. Once again, that teachers may be accurately assessing the accuracy and validity of these shows is beside the point; if their students are watching these shows in large numbers, teachers must adjust to this reality and seek ways to use these shows to complement (if not bolster) their own teaching materials.

Conclusion

The proliferation of digital media sources for news and information within the high schools can no longer be ignored as just another passing fad. With the vast majority of students enjoying access to the Internet at home and at school, the new media reaches literally everywhere. To their credit, parents have kept up with their teenagers' habits to a degree: 87 percent of parents of online teens are e-mail or Internet users. Most teachers are also Internet users, but they have not been so quick to embrace the new technology as a means of gathering news or information. As a consequence, a generation gap concerning the digital media may have infected the classroom itself, as teachers and students now consume news in markedly different ways.

Perhaps the most significant new trend in student digital media use concerns their dissemination habits. Not only do nearly a third of high school students read blogs for news and information at least once per week, but thanks to MySpace.com and Facebook.com, students are themselves bloggers. Nearly a third (32 percent) also say they post messages online at least weekly, and 10 percent say they do so every day. Clearly, the digital media have created a generation of bloggers who express opinions and disseminate those opinions widely: 44 percent of the students surveyed say they participate in online discussions and chat groups at least once per week.

The implications of this new revolution are potentially significant. When their participation in the media was limited to high school newspapers, magazines, and the like, students were at the mercy of journalism advisors who directed the project and edited their materials, and they were at the mercy of principals willing to censor stories if their content was deemed offensive. But as do-it-yourself bloggers, students now serve as their own editors and their own publishers, making editorial and publication decisions outside the reach of school authorities. If students now play roles in journalism formerly reserved to adults, they presumably are more sensitive to editors' and publishers' rights to disseminate their materials freely. Are the bloggers and new media users of today more likely to favor free expression and free press rights than other students? We take that final question up in chapter 5.

Notes

1. "A Message from Mayor Harger," *Village Views* 37, no. 2 (June–July 2006): 1.

2. Sherry Saavedra, "How Much Space to Give MySpace Users," *San Diego Union-Tribune*, June 4, 2006, www.signonsandiego.com/news/education/20060604-9999-1n4myspace.html (accessed 1 August 2007).

3. See, e.g., *Chambers v. Roosevelt Union Free School Dist.*, 689 N.Y.S.2d. 171 (App. Div. 2d Dep't 1999); *Marshall v. Courtland Enlarged City School Dist.*, 697 N.Y.S.2d 395 (App. Div. 3d Dep't 1999).

4. Michael Beder, "Free Speech Fight Hits Kirkwood High," *St. Louis Post-Dispatch*, May 24, 2006, www.stltoday.com/stltoday/news/stories.nsf/education/story/CD0 CE6B1B78A488D86257178001A2DDB (accessed on July 5, 2006).

5. Beder, "Free Speech Fight."

6. Saavedra, "How Much Space," 1.

7. Hope Anderson, "The MySpace Case," *Daily News* (Longview, Washington), January 21, 2006, www.tdn.com/articles/2006/01/22/top_story/news01.txt (accessed 15 September 2007).

8. See Lynne Lancaster and David Stillman, *When Generations Collide: Who They Are. Why They Clash. How to Solve the Generational Problem at Work* (New York: Collins, 2003); Neil Howe, William Strauss, and R. J. Matson, *Millennials Rising: The Next Generation* (New York: Vintage, 2000); Cliff Zukin et al., *A New Engagement? Political Participation, Civic Life, and the Changing American Citizen* (New York: Oxford, 2006).

9. See Wendy Chun and Thomas Keenan, eds., *New Media, Old Media: Interrogating the Digital Revolution* (New York: Routledge, 2003), for an exploration of the tensions of "old media" and "new media" in the current digital culture. Many believe "new media" defines a field of academic study; others counter that the phrase "new media" also includes some forms of media art, creative industries, computer game theory, and so forth.

10. Lev Manovich, *The Language of New Media* (Cambridge, MA: MIT Press, 2001).

11. See Robert Harrow, *No Place to Hide: Behind the Scenes of Our Emerging Surveillance Society* (New York: Free Press, 2005).

12. See "World Internet Users, November 2007," Internet World Stats, www.internetworldstats.com/stats.htm (accessed 25 November 2007).

13. Geoff Keighly, "The Secrets of Drudge Inc.," CNNMoney.com, April 1, 2003, http://money.cnn.com/magazines/business2/business2_archive/2003/04/01/339822/index.htm (accessed 20 September 2007).

14. Glenn Reynolds, *An Army of Davids: How Markets and Technology Empower Ordinary People to Beat Big Media, Big Government and Other Goliaths* (Nashville, TN: Nelson Current, 2006).

15. At the time of this writing, the *Wall Street Journal* was one of the few major daily newspapers to offer access only to regular subscribers to the paper version of the newspaper or to those willing to pay a yearly fee for Web access only. Meanwhile, other newspapers, including the *New York Times*, had spoken publicly of the possibility that access charges might be coming soon. And almost every major newspaper charged readers wishing to view earlier articles from the newspaper's archives.

16. "The *Times* after the Storm: Jayson Blair, Howell Raines, and the Rest of Us," *Columbia Journalism Review* 42 (July 1, 2003): 14.

17. Reynolds is quoted in Nicholas Lemann, "The Wayward Press: Amateur Hour," *New Yorker*, August 7 and 14, 2006, 44.

18. Lemann, "The Wayward Press," 44.

19. Amanda Lenhart and Susannah Fox, "'Bloggers': A Portrait of the Internet's New Storytellers" (report of the Pew Internet & American Life Project, July 19, 2006), 1, www.pewinternet.org/pdfs/PIP%20Bloggers%20Report%20July%2019%202006.pdf (accessed 1 March 2008).

20. Lenhart and Fox, "'Bloggers': A Portrait," 11.

21. Anita Ramasastry, "Can Schools Punish Students for Posting Offensive Content on MySpace and Similar Sites?" *Findlaw's Modern Practice: Cyberlaw*, May 1, 2006, 1, http://practice.findlaw.comramasastry/20060501.html (accessed 1 March 2008).

22. Janet Kornblum, "Teens Hang Out at MySpace," USAToday.com, July 12, 2006. www.usatoday.com/tech/news/2006-1-08-myspace-teens_xhtm?loc=intersticialskip (accessed 1 March 2008).

23. 521 U.S. 844 (1997) (emphasizing the legitimacy and importance of protecting children from harmful materials on the Internet, so long as the regulations do not unduly restrict the freedom of adults to communicate with other adults).

24. 458 U.S. 747 (1982) (upholding a state law prohibiting the distribution of materials depicting sexual performances by children under sixteen).

25. Steven Levy, *The Perfect Thing: How the iPod Shuffles Commerce, Culture, and Coolness.* New York: Simon & Schuster, 2006.

26. See "Parents & Teens Survey: Data for October 26–November 28, 2004, Princeton Survey Research Associates International, for the Pew Internet & American Life Project." www.pewinternet.org/PPF/r/152/report_display.asp (accessed 1 March 2008).

27. This is according to a recent survey conducted by the National Conference on Citizenship.

5

The Digital Media and Attitudes about Free Expression Rights

I N CHAPTER 4, WE DETAILED HOW THE DIGITAL MEDIA have had a profound impact on American habits today. Individuals now spend a significant amount of time using digital media forms to communicate with others, to publish their thoughts and ideas, and to seek out various types of information and news about what is happening in their communities, their states, the nation, and the world.

The digital media have changed the news environment in America. Internet news sites provide considerable detail about events both past and present. They provide real-time updates of news and events as they occur, with not only text but also pictures and live video streams. They allow users to proactively seek out the kind of information they are looking for, whether it's news about business, sports, the day's events, such as the war in Iraq, or the latest public opinion polls. These news sites, as well as the sites of Internet service providers, often include data archives of past news stories, so they may be used not only to obtain information about current events but also to do research.

Moreover, through online discussions, chat rooms, and blogs, the digital media facilitate user participation in both reporting and commenting on events. With a computer and an Internet connection, anyone can provide information, opinions, ideas, and comments about the news of the day, public policy debates, recent movies, vacation experiences, and the like. In short, these new media have empowered average people to readily publish their thoughts and opinions for the rest of the world to see.

To what extent is the revolution spurred by the digital media having an influence on Americans' attitudes about the First Amendment and free expression rights? Recall that the First Amendment is supposed to protect the public's use of these digital media, as it does more traditional forms of media.

High school students are especially susceptible to the influence of the communications revolution. They are at a life cycle stage when they are likely to be influenced not only by their parents, friends, and educational experiences but also by their direct experiences with these digital media. Teenagers are even more likely to publish their thoughts through digital media than older Americans. As we reported earlier, virtually all of today's high school students access the Internet, signaling the imminent end to the digital divide through the process of generational replacement.

Indeed, it is likely that the impact of the digital media is disproportionately falling on the younger generation of high school–age Americans. High school–age citizens are in their formative years when they develop habits about media usage, news reliance, and the use of technologies. They are also at a critical stage in the political socialization process, when strong attitudes about democratic values are formed and hardened. The way in which those in their formative years use digital media is likely to influence the future of America in many ways. With more opportunities now than ever before to access news and publish one's own ideas, are younger people who use the digital media more supportive and appreciative of the basic democratic principle that allows them this access to and forum for communication?

This chapter examines the role of the digital media in relation to support for the First Amendment's provision for free expression rights. Do student users of these digital media also experience a heightened interest in news? Do these media, which are more accessible to the younger generation, lead students to greater appreciation and support for free expression rights? Perhaps more significantly, do students who make use of the Internet in order to publish their opinions through blogs or chat groups maintain a greater appreciation for press rights?

To answer these questions, we use the FOFA 2006 data, which classify students into a number of different categories based on their utilization of the digital media, and then compare those distinct groups with responses to questions measuring use of the news and support for freedom of expression. The groupings of students are as follows:

1. **Use of Internet for news:** The FOFA 2006 survey asked students, "How often, if at all, do you get news and information from online or Internet sources in general—every day, several times a week, about once a week, less than once a week, or never?" For the analysis in this chapter, we have

created three groupings of students based on use of the Internet for news, which include (1) frequent users (use at least several times, representing 31 percent of all high school students); (2) infrequent users (use once a week or less, representing 40 percent of all students); and (3) nonusers (have never used, representing 29 percent).

2. **Use of blogs to get information:** The FOFA 2006 survey asks a question that begins with the following: "Short for 'weblogs,' blogs are defined as online journals in which people post diary entries about their personal experiences and opinions to be read online by others. Examples of blog collections include Myspace.com and Facebook.com." FOFA 2006 then queried as follows: "How often, if at all, do you get news and information from blogs—every day, several times a week, about once a week, less than once a week, or never?" For the analysis in this chapter, we have created three groupings of students, which include (1) frequent bloggers (use at least several times, representing 20 percent of all high school students); (2) infrequent bloggers (use once a week or less, representing 28 percent of all students); and (3) nonbloggers (have never used, representing 52 percent).

3. **Participation in online discussions:** FOFA 2006 also asked students, "Now thinking about what you do online, how often, if at all, do you use the Internet, the World Wide Web, or an online service to participate in online discussions or chat groups—every day, several times a week, about once a week, less than once a week, or never?" For the analysis in this chapter, we have created three groupings of students, which include (1) frequent participants in online discussions (participate at least several times, representing 19 percent of all high school students); (2) infrequent participants (participate once a week or less, representing 31 percent of all students); and (3) nonparticipants (never participate, representing 40 percent).

4. **Posting material to blogs:** FOFA 2006 asked, "Now thinking about what you do online, how often, if at all, do you use the Internet, the World Wide Web, or an online service to post messages or opinions to online columns or blogs that may be read by the general public—every day, several times a week, about once a week, less than once a week, or never?" For the analysis in this chapter, we have created three groupings of students, which include (1) frequent blog posters (use at least several times, representing 21 percent of all high school students); (2) infrequent blog posters (use once a week or less, representing 28 percent of all students); and (3) nonblog-posters (have never used, representing 51 percent).

The first two sets of classifications provide a nomenclature for evaluating how accessing digital media as consumers might influence attitudes about free expression rights, while the last two, which indicate the level of publishing activity in chats and blogs, examine the relationship between self-publishing in digital form and free expression rights.

Are Students Who Use Digital Media to Get News and Information More Supportive of Freedom of Expression?

The availability of news and information through online sources has transformed the way that people receive and access information. Users can query the World Wide Web through search engines for information about virtually any topic. They can use network TV websites, the sites of Internet service providers such as Yahoo! and Google, or the sites of national and local newspapers to get up-to-the minute news about current events or to retrieve news about a particular topic of interest. Further, the proliferation of blogs also makes available a tremendous amount of personal opinion and commentary. The ability to passively or actively get news, information, or the opinions of others is greater today due to this new medium than it ever was in the past.

Our research, then, poses these important questions: Do those who use online sources for news and information develop a greater appreciation for free expression rights? Similarly, do those who use blogs, which are primarily "new," or digital, media that provide opinion and commentary, come to develop a deeper appreciation for free speech and free press rights? In short, does exposure to the wealth of information, news, commentary, and opinion on the Internet lead to a greater appreciation for enjoying access to the vast flow of ideas accessible through the Internet?

We now provide answers to these questions for the four sets of free expression items: (1) does the First Amendment go too far in the rights it guarantees? (2) does the press in particular have too much freedom? (3) do you support any of the five dimensions of free expression? and (4) to what extent is the First Amendment taken for granted?

Does the First Amendment Go Too Far?

Table 5.1 proves there is a relationship between the frequency of use of online information sources and disagreement with the general notion that the First Amendment goes too far in the rights it guarantees. More frequent users of media websites and Internet service providers exhibit greater resistance to the suggestion that the First Amendment provides excessive freedom. However, our data also find that blogging has no apparent influence on this more generalized orientation toward First Amendment freedoms. Table 5.1 also shows that even when many demographic and other factors are controlled, those who are frequent users of the Internet to gather news are most likely to

Table 5.1
Does the First Amendment Go Too Far in the Rights It Guarantees?
(And Internet Use for News)

	Percentage Disagreeing	
	Unadjusted (%)	Adjusted (%)
How often do you get news online?		
Frequently	42*	41*
Infrequently	37*	38
Never	30	32
How often do you get news from blogs?		
Frequently	37	33
Infrequently	37	35
Never	35	37

Source: FOFA 2006. Adjusted percentages are obtained from a multinomial logit model that controls for participation in specific courses, extracurricular activities with news content, use of the Internet for news consumption, and other factors such as gender, race or ethnicity, school type, self-reported GPA, type of Internet access, U.S. citizenship, self-reported economic class, and grade enrolled in at the time of the survey. For complete multinomial logit results, see appendix C, table C.2. An * indicates a statistically significant difference at the 0.05 level of confidence.

disagree with the statement that the First Amendment goes too far in the rights it guarantees. However, even once important factors are controlled, the relationship between views of the First Amendment and the use of blogs for gathering information is inverse and weak.[1]

Does the Press in America Have Too Much Freedom?

When it comes to free press rights in particular, high school students who use online news sources are much more likely to feel that the press has either "the right amount" or "too little" freedom in America to do what it wants. As shown in table 5.2, 46 percent of nonusers say the press has the right amount or too little freedom; 52 percent of infrequent users feel that way, with fully 58 percent of frequent online users saying this. Those who use blogs as a source of information are similarly (and statistically) more convinced that the press does not have excessive freedoms in America: 48 percent of nonblog users, 57 percent of infrequent blog users, and 56 percent of frequent blog users do not believe that the press has excessive freedom in America, suggesting a relationship between the frequency of using blogs for information and views of press freedoms. However, once observed factors are controlled, many of these differences between blog users and nonusers are eliminated.

These findings demonstrate that there is, in fact, a significant relationship between use of online news sources for information and the opinion that the press is not given more rights than it deserves. Use of these sources appears to

Table 5.2
Views of Press Freedom in America and Internet Use for News, 2006

	Overall, Does the Press in America Have . . .							
	Too Much Freedom		Too Little Freedom		About Right		Don't Know	
	Unadjusted (%)	Adjusted (%)	Unadjusted (%)	Adjusted (%)	Unadjusted (%)	Adjusted (%)	Unadjusted (%)	Adjusted (%)
How often do you get news online?								
Frequently	30	31	13	11	45	46	12	11
Infrequently	30	31	12	10	40	45	19	14
Never	29	29	10	10	36	38	26	22
How often do you get news from blogs?								
Frequently	28	28	14	13	42	42	15	17
Infrequently	27	28	13	12	44	43	17	17
Never	31	32	9	9	39	42	20	17

Source: FOFA 2006. Adjusted percentages are obtained from a multinomial logit model that controls for participation in specific courses, extracurricular activities with news content, use of the Internet for news consumption, and other factors such as gender, race or ethnicity, school type, self-reported GPA, type of Internet access, U.S. citizenship, self-reported economic class, and grade enrolled in at the time of the survey. For complete multinomial logit results, see appendix C, table C.3.

engender the sense that the press is properly fitted with the resources it needs to carry out its role in providing coverage of events effectively. The active use of the digital media in gathering information appears to enhance feelings among high school students that the press is not overstepping its bounds. In contrast, these findings also suggest a very weak, though positive, correlation between the use of blogs as a source of information and the opinion that the press is not given more rights than it deserves.

Dimensions of Support for Free Expression

In chapter 3 we presented five specific items, which we argued represented various dimensions of support for free expression rights. These items were presented to students in the form of agree/disagree statements. The items include the following:

1. People should be allowed to express unpopular opinions.
2. People should be allowed to burn or deface the American flag as a political statement.
3. Musicians should be allowed to sing songs with lyrics that others might find offensive.
4. Newspapers should be allowed to publish freely without government approval of a story.
5. High school students should be allowed to report controversial issues in their student newspapers without the approval of school authorities.

Table 5.3 depicts the findings for these items across the "online use of news" and "use of blogs" categories. The table demonstrates several important dynamics. First, while frequency of online use of news and frequency of use of blogs for news both share a positive and statistically significant relationship with most of the free expression items, the former tends to share a stronger relationship. That is, more regular use of the Internet to get information is more highly associated with support for free expression than is more regular use of blogs to get information. The data indicate that something about the experience of searching for and gathering information from media websites and Internet service providers is substantively different from (and more enriching with respect to support for free expression rights than) getting information from blogs. Perhaps this difference lies in the nature of the websites compared to the blogs. Those using websites are more likely to be seeking news and information, while those reading blogs are searching for opinions and seeking to read others' commentary. While both necessarily seem to lead to more support for expression rights, the former may be a more serious news-seeking experience for many

Table 5.3

Attitudes about Free Expression by Use of Online News and Blogs, 2006

First Amendment Attitudes

(%)	Unpopular Opinions (1)		Flag Burning (2)		Offensive Song Lyrics (3)		Papers Publishing Freely (4)		Student Paper Issues (5)	
	Unadjusted (%)	Adjusted (%)	Unadjusted (%)	Adjusted (%)	Unadjusted (%)	Adjusted (%)	Unadjusted (%)	Adjusted (%)	Unadjusted (%)	Adjusted (%)
All high schoolers										
Agree	85	88	15	15	69	70	55	55	64	65
Disagree	7	6	76	78	23	23	35	36	25	25
No opinion	7	6	8	7	8	6	10	9	11	9
Online frequent users										
Agree	90	91	18	17	75	73	62	61	72	71
Disagree	6	5	74	77	22	23	32	33	22	23
No opinion	4	3	6	5	5	4	6	5	6	6
Online infrequent users										
Agree	87	90	15	15	68	71	53	56	63	67
Disagree	7	6	78	79	25	24	37	36	26	25
No opinion	6	4	7	6	7	5	9	7	10	8
Online nonusers										
Agree	80	85	13	13	64	69	48	51	57	61
Disagree	7	7	75	78	24	23	37	37	26	26
No opinion	12	8	12	9	12	9	16	12	17	13

Frequent blog users										
Agree	89	88	18	14	72	69	56	52	69	65
Disagree	6	6	75	79	22	23	36	38	23	25
No opinion	5	6	7	14	6	7	8	10	8	10
Infrequent blog users										
Agree	86	87	16	14	68	68	55	54	64	64
Disagree	7	6	77	79	25	25	36	36	26	26
No opinion	6	7	7	7	7	7	9	9	10	10
Blog nonusers										
Agree	84	88	15	15	68	71	52	56	62	66
Disagree	7	6	77	77	24	22	36	36	25	28
No opinion	9	6	9	7	8	6	11	9	12	9

Source: FOFA 2006. Adjusted percentages are obtained from a multinomial logit model that controls for participation in specific courses, extracurricular activities with news content, use of the Internet for news consumption, and other factors such as gender, race or ethnicity, school type, self-reported GPA, type of Internet access, U.S. citizenship, self-reported economic class, and grade enrolled in at the time of the survey. For complete multinomial logit results, see appendix C, tables C.6 to C.10.

consumers, and this may explain why there seems to be a more positive relationship between views of the First Amendment and online website use.

Second, the two items that specifically reference press rights offer the greatest attitudinal differences. Of frequent online news users, 62 percent say that newspapers should be allowed to publish freely without government approval of a story, compared to 48 percent of those who do not use the Internet to get news—a very large, 14-percentage-point difference. Similarly, 72 percent of frequent online news users say that students should be allowed to publish stories in the school newspaper without the approval of school authorities, while 57 percent of those who do not go online agree, representing a fifteen-point difference. Even though many of these large differences are mitigated once other observed factors, such as gender, self-reported GPA, and race or ethnicity, are accounted for, a statistically significant relationship between online news use and support for press rights remains evident. The more frequent use of online sources for news, then, seems to have greater influence on positive attitudes about the press per se, compared to other manifestations of free expression.

Therefore, online use of news (more so than use of blogs for news) and attitudes relating more closely to press rights (more so than speech rights) depict the greatest statistical relationship between digital media behavior and free expression attitudes. For item 1, which taps the more abstract, generalized opinions of free expression, those who frequently get news online (90 percent) and those who frequently use blogs to get information (89 percent) are significantly more likely to agree that individuals should be allowed to express unpopular opinions than those who infrequently or never use these new media to get news and information, though the vast majority of all high school students, independently of their media use, are supportive of this viewpoint. As expected, once observed factors are controlled, adjusted percentages suggests a slightly smaller difference between those who use these media sources frequently and those who do not.

For the flag burning (item 2) and offensive song lyrics (item 3) items, it is clear that frequent online news users are significantly more likely to offer pro–free expression responses, even once observed factors are controlled. Those who frequently use blogs to get information are less apt to hold pro–free expression rights attitudes than online news users.

To What Extent Is the First Amendment Taken for Granted?

Table 5.4 shows that online news users and readers of blogs are more likely to have formed an opinion as to whether or not they personally take the First Amendment for granted than those who do not use these media sources for

Table 5.4
Views of Rights Guaranteed by the First Amendment and Internet Activities, 2006

| | Are the Rights Guaranteed by the First Amendment Something You . . . | | | | | |
| | Personally Think About | | Take for Granted | | Don't Know | |
	Unadjusted (%)	Adjusted (%)	Unadjusted (%)	Adjusted (%)	Unadjusted (%)	Adjusted (%)
How often do you get news online?						
Frequently	31	32	45	43	25	24
Infrequently	23	26	44	44	33	29
Never	20	20	38	41	43	39
How often do you get news from blogs?						
Frequently	26	22	44	45	30	32
Infrequently	25	24	43	44	32	32
Never	23	25	41	42	36	33

Source: FOFA 2006. Adjusted percentages are obtained from a multinomial logit model that controls for participation in specific courses, extracurricular activities with news content, use of the Internet for news consumption, and other factors such as gender, race or ethnicity, school type, self-reported GPA, type of Internet access, U.S. citizenship, self-reported economic class, and grade enrolled in at the time of the survey. For complete multinomial logit results, see appendix C, table C.5.

information, even once other factors are considered. Note that these differences are more pronounced for online news users than for blog users. The formation of opinions through the use of these digital media, however, is split evenly between the "personally think about" and "take for granted" responses. Students who use these new media are more thoughtful about the First Amendment; yet, their experiences in using online news and blogs do not seem to direct their attitudes in a particular direction. Controlling for other possible confounding factors does not change this story.

Are Students Who Use New Media to Publish More Supportive of the First Amendment?

As we suggested at the outset of this chapter (and have done throughout this book), the digital media not only open up access to a plethora of news and information sources but also dramatically extend the ability to publish. And as we reported in chapter 4, many high school students are taking advantage of these publishing opportunities. The question we address in this section is as follows: are those who are taking advantage of the digital media by publishing becoming more supportive and appreciative of the constitutional principles that protect the rights of expression?[2]

Does the First Amendment Go Too Far?

As demonstrated in table 5.5, those who are frequent users of digital media to express their own opinions are least likely to disagree that the First Amendment goes too far in the rights it guarantees, and are the most likely to have offered an opinion, even once observed factors are controlled. This suggests that those who use digital media technologies to express their opinions are more supportive of, and are more likely to have formed an opinion about, the First Amendment than those who do not use these digital media sources frequently.

Does the Press in America Have Too Much Freedom?

On the issue of whether the press has an excess of freedom, the data show, as displayed in table 5.6, that participation in online discussions and the posting of material to blogs has a positive and statistically significant relationship with the feeling that the press does not have too much freedom to do what it wants. Specifically, 49 percent and 48 percent, respectively, of those who do not chat online and do not post material to blogs say the press has either the "right

Table 5.5
Does the First Amendment Go Too Far in the Rights It Guarantees for Internet Activities?

	Agree		Disagree		Don't Know	
	Unadjusted (%)	Adjusted (%)	Unadjusted (%)	Adjusted (%)	Unadjusted (%)	Adjusted (%)
How often do you use chat rooms?						
Frequently	48	49	34	34	17	17
Infrequently	45	47	39	38	17	15
Never	41	45	37	36	21	18
How often do you use blogs?						
Frequently	49	47	35	38	15	15
Infrequently	45	45	38	38	17	16
Never	43	47	42	34	21	18

Source: FOFA 2006. Adjusted percentages are obtained from a multinomial logit model that controls for participation in specific courses, extracurricular activities with news content, use of the Internet for news consumption, and other factors such as gender, race or ethnicity, school type, self-reported GPA, type of Internet access, U.S. citizenship, self-reported economic class, and grade enrolled in at the time of the survey. For complete multinomial logit results, see appendix C, table C.2.

Table 5.6
Views of Press Freedom in America and Internet Activities, 2006

	Overall, Does the Press in America Have . . .							
	Too Much Freedom		Too Little Freedom		About Right		Don't Know	
	Unadjusted (%)	Adjusted (%)	Unadjusted (%)	Adjusted (%)	Unadjusted (%)	Adjusted (%)	Unadjusted (%)	Adjusted (%)
How often do you use chat rooms?								
Frequently	29	30	12	11	42	42	16	16
Infrequently	28	29	13	12	42	43	17	16
Never	31	31	9	10	40	42	20	18
How often do you use blogs?								
Frequently	29	30	15	13	41	41	15	15
Infrequently	27	28	12	12	44	44	16	16
Never	31	31	9	10	39	41	20	18

Source: FOFA 2006. Adjusted percentages are obtained from a multinomial logit model that controls for participation in specific courses, extracurricular activities with news content, use of the Internet for news consumption, and other factors such as gender, race or ethnicity, school type, self-reported GPA, type of Internet access, U.S. citizenship, self-reported economic class, and grade enrolled in at the time of the survey. For complete multinomial logit results, see appendix C, table C.3.

amount" or "too little" freedom in America. By contrast, 54 percent of those who do participate in online conversations and 56 percent of those who post material to blogs offer this opinion about the press's freedom. Those engaging in online publishing are, in fact, more sensitive to restrictions on the behavior of the press, even once observed confounding factors are controlled. The fact that individuals who publish their ideas through online conversations and blogs are more favorable toward press freedoms suggests that engaging in digital publishing may have the effect of promoting support for press freedoms.

Dimensions of Support for Free Expression

We now turn to findings with respect to the possible effects of online publishing on support for the various dimensions of free expression, as measured through the five agree/disagree statements. Table 5.7 demonstrates that frequency of engaging in online discussions shares a relationship with most of these dimensions of free expression. Generally, the greater the use of chat rooms and online discussions, the more students are willing to support free expression rights. And the relationships are similar in magnitude; that is, the percentage improvement in agreement, from those who do not chat to those who are frequent chatters, is in the range of five to eight points, all of which is statistically significant without any confounding factors controlled, and from one to five points when these factors are controlled, in some cases showing a wider gap.

There is also a clear influence of publishing through postings on blogs. The more frequently students engage in posting material on blogs, the more they say they support free expression across all five of the dimensions that we measured. The magnitude of the relationships appears highest on the press-specific items (items 4 and 5), where the spread between those who do not post and those who frequently post is nine percentage points, even once observed factors are controlled. This suggests a very strong relationship between blogging and support for free expression and media rights.

Again, the experience of using these digital media to publish materials does appear to have a corresponding positive influence on heightened support for free expression rights. The act of publishing makes students more appreciative and supportive of free expression, particularly as it relates to press rights. These findings suggest that as students continue to engage in online publishing, they may come to better appreciate free expression rights.

To What Extent Is the First Amendment Taken for Granted?

Finally, table 5.8 addresses the question of whether online publishing leads students to be more reflective of their First Amendment rights. Two findings

Table 5.7
Attitudes about Free Expression and Internet Activities, 2006

	First Amendment Attitudes									
	Unpopular Opinions (1)		Flag Burning (2)		Offensive Song Lyrics (3)		Papers Publishing Freely (4)		Student Paper Issues (5)	
(%)	Unadjusted (%)	Adjusted (%)	Unadjusted (%)	Adjusted (%)	Unadjusted (%)	Adjusted (%)	Unadjusted (%)	Adjusted (%)	Unadjusted (%)	Adjusted (%)
All high schoolers										
Agree	85	88	15	15	69	70	55	55	64	66
Disagree	7	6	76	78	23	23	35	36	25	25
No opinion	7	6	8	7	8	6	10	9	11	9
Frequent chat room users										
Agree	89	89	18	15	73	73	57	55	67	67
Disagree	6	5	76	79	22	21	35	36	24	24
No opinion	6	5	6	6	6	5	9	9	9	9
Infrequent chat room users										
Agree	86	89	17	15	69	72	56	57	65	67
Disagree	7	6	75	48	23	22	34	35	24	24
No opinion	6	4	8	6	7	6	9	8	10	9
Chat room nonusers										
Agree	83	86	13	14	65	68	52	54	61	64
Disagree	8	7	77	78	25	24	37	36	26	26
No opinion	9	7	10	8	9	7	12	9	13	10

Table 5.8
Views of Rights Guaranteed by the First Amendment and Internet Activities, 2006

| | Are the Rights Guaranteed by the First Amendment Something You . . . . | | | | | |
| | Personally Think About | | Take for Granted | | Don't Know | |
	Unadjusted (%)	Adjusted (%)	Unadjusted (%)	Adjusted (%)	Unadjusted (%)	Adjusted (%)
How often do you use chat rooms?						
Frequently	25	24	43	43	32	33
Infrequently	25	24	42	43	33	33
Never	13	24	42	43	45	33
How often do you use blogs?						
Frequently	28	29	42	41	30	30
Infrequently	25	26	43	43	31	31
Never	22	23	41	43	36	34

Source: FOFA 2006. Adjusted percentages are obtained from a multinomial logit model that controls for participation in specific courses, extracurricular activities with news content, use of the Internet for news consumption, and other factors such as gender, race or ethnicity, school type, self-reported GPA, type of Internet access, U.S. citizenship, self-reported economic class, and grade enrolled in at the time of the survey. For complete multinomial logit results, see appendix C, table C.5.

Frequent blog posters										
Agree	89	90	21	21	74	76	59	61	70	71
Disagree	6	6	71	72	21	20	33	32	22	22
No opinion	5	4	7	7	5	5	8	7	8	7
Infrequent blog posters										
Agree	88	89	18	18	71	74	57	59	67	69
Disagree	6	6	76	75	23	21	34	34	25	23
No opinion	5	4	7	7	7	5	8	7	9	8
Blog nonposters										
Agree	84	87	13	12	66	67	50	52	61	63
Disagree	8	7	78	80	25	25	37	38	27	26
No opinion	9	7	9	7	9	8	12	10	13	11

Source: FOFA 2006. Adjusted percentages are obtained from a multinomial logit model that controls for participation in specific courses, extracurricular activities with news content, use of the Internet for news consumption, and other factors such as gender, race or ethnicity, school type, self-reported GPA, type of Internet access, U.S. citizenship, self-reported economic class, and grade enrolled in at the time of the survey. For complete multinomial logit results, see appendix C, tables C.6 to C.10.

are noteworthy in this regard. First, similar to the findings presented earlier in this chapter regarding use of online material, more frequent blog posting and more frequent online chatting are related to having an opinion and thinking about the issue of whether or not one takes his or her rights for granted. For example, 45 percent of those who never participate in online discussions say they do not know how to answer this question, compared to 32 percent of those who frequently participate in chat rooms. Second, at least with respect to posting material on blogs, it does appear that frequency of this behavior leads to the development of an attitude toward more personally thinking about First Amendment rights: 22 percent of nonbloggers say they personally think about their rights, while 28 percent of frequent bloggers say the same.

It is important to note here, however, that controlling confounding factors mitigates the relationship between online chatting and views of the rights guaranteed by the First Amendment. Specifically, once observable factors are controlled, frequency of chat room use is unrelated to students' views of the rights guaranteed by the First Amendment.

Conclusion

Naturally, one would expect the beneficiaries of freedom to stand tall among its greatest defenders. High school students, who must navigate a litany of re-strictions and rules every day both at home and at school, should be first and foremost among them. Yet, FOFA 2004 revealed some sobering truths about high school students in particular: they tend to be less tolerant of First Amendment expression than school teachers, school principals, and even the adult population as a whole in many instances. FOFA 2004 revealed that stu-dents who participate in student media tend to be more supportive of these freedoms. Unfortunately, so few students participate (no more than 10 per-cent participate in any school-authorized media activity) that a less tolerant and more apathetic ethos prevailed in the nation's high schools: Nearly three-fourths of students in 2004 either said they didn't know how they felt about the First Amendment or that they took it for granted.

The digital media revolution of recent years has influenced the way many institutions in democracy work. Members of Congress trade e-mails with constituents and accept campaign contributions via the Internet; Supreme Court opinions can be distributed across the globe within seconds and invite criticisms and controversy within minutes; the president of the United States is the subject of thousands of online diaries chronicling his every move. What about high school students, who in many cases are even more technologically savvy than the adults? What type of impact has the digital media revolution

had on them, and more specifically, how, if at all, has it affected their appreciation and support for free expression rights? FOFA 2006 offered numerous
ways of measuring the degree to which new media users, be they those who
consume online media or who participate in and create new media, tend to
support the very First Amendment freedoms that buttress their activities.

As it turns out, the more intense digital media users are more aware of the
role they play in the so-called "marketplace of ideas," and they are more likely
to defend the freedom of that marketplace than those who interact with digital media less often. In assessing those who use the digital media as a source
of news and information, data from FOFA 2006 revealed that a significant and
positive relationship exists between those who use online sources for information and news and the perception that the press is not given more rights
than it deserves. Beyond just support for free press rights, those who more
regularly use the Internet to get information tend to be highly associated with
support for all sorts of free expression rights. Certainly, not all Internet sites
are the same. In contrast, we found that those who rely on blogs for news do
not exhibit the same level of support for free expression rights as those who
gather information regularly from more "established" Internet websites. Perhaps that's because they're searching for opinions rather than searching for
"news" per se. Still, the overall connection between Internet usage and support
for free expression rights appears to be a strong one.

What about the millions of bloggers who create online diaries?[3] Their numbers are not small: thanks to MySpace.com and other social-networking sites
that are growing substantially, it has never been easier for the nation's high
school students to e-mail, chat online, and post their opinions in a place
where the public can consume them. Certainly, FOFA 2006 reveals that bloggers, as well as those who participate in online discussions, tend to think the
press in America does not have enough freedom to publish. In fact, online
publishers, who now number in the tens of millions, are more sensitive to restrictions on the behavior of the press in general.

Moreover, the more frequently students engage in activities such as posting
materials on blogs, the more likely they are to support all manner of free expression across the five separate dimensions studied in FOFA 2006. And finally, with regard to the issue of apathy toward the First Amendment—a measure that registered so low that it startled many educators when they first
learned about it in 2004—it appears that the more frequent bloggers tend to
develop an attitude that includes more personal thought about First Amendment rights in general. Thus, student bloggers are leading a revolution many
of us should be familiar with: it is a revolution that supports free expression
rights in general and free press rights in particular.

What are the implications of this new media movement on democracy in
general and on our rights as Americans in particular? This much is certain:

high school students are especially likely to be socialized in ways that promote democracy and celebrate the rights and liberties of all Americans if they engage in an activity that serves as a manifestation of those rights in practice. Student newspapers and other more traditional student media once provided that outlet; unfortunately, they tend to be inherently limited by several factors, including (1) their dependence on advisors and principals to support them with resources, and (2) their dependence on school authorities to help them distribute news to fellow students and the school community as a whole on a regular basis. That dynamic places principals in a position to censor or discourage certain news items, even when they are important and newsworthy. Some principals, caught between a rock and a hard place, may choose to influence (or, in extreme cases, outright censor) the content of student newspapers to avoid the risk of angering parents, superintendents, and others. The adage "better safe than sorry" may be practical, but it does little to promote learning about the value of freedom of expression in the nation's high schools.

In 2006, the more apt adage reads, "If you can't beat 'em, join 'em." High school students have apparently done exactly that, reading and accessing Internet news, then becoming their own editors and publishers through sites such as Myspace.com. School officials have reason to be wary: they cannot condone the dissemination of pornographic materials and other irresponsible activity on the Internet any more than they can condone it in student newspapers or magazines. But the vast majority of what's found on blogs falls within the core protections of the First Amendment, and students who post material online are direct beneficiaries of this robust marketplace of ideas. Those same students who go online and read about news or publish their opinions about it are also among the leading defenders of free expression rights. More effective forms of civic education cannot easily be found.

Of course, principals and educational reformers may fairly ask the question, how can high school officials encourage freedom of expression activities that offer such an effective civic education, while at the same time protecting their students (and themselves) from those who would abuse these privileges? We take up that final issue in chapter 6.

Notes

1. For more information on the factors controlled and the types of models estimated, see chapter 3 and appendix C.

2. It may also be the case, however, that the positive relationships we below are driven not by the effect of blogging or using chat rooms to publish one's own opinions but, instead, by an intervening factor that drives both attitudes toward the First Amendment and students' use of blogs or chat rooms to publish their own opinions. In other words,

there may be some positive self-selection involved in determining attitudes toward the First Amendment and participation in new digital media technologies.

3. The National Conference on Citizenship estimates that there are over eighteen million bloggers in a recent report on Internet use and civic engagement. See *America's Civic Health Index 2007. Renewed Engagement: Building on America's Civic Core*, National Conference on Citizenship, www.ncoc.net/pdf/civicindex.pdf (accessed 4 October 2007).

6

Putting the First Amendment First: Policy Implications and the Future of Freedom of Expression

For nearly 220 years, the First Amendment's guarantee of free expression rights has offered a beacon of light to nations around the world. It serves as a continuing symbol of the U.S. political system's formal commitment to protect a free and robust marketplace of ideas, which includes tolerance for dissent against the government's own policies. Unfortunately, words and deeds rarely align in this context. For the better part of the twentieth century, the former Soviet Union provided in its own constitution of "fundamental law" that its citizens were guaranteed "freedom of speech" and "of the press."[1] Prior to the 2003 overthrow of Saddam Hussein's regime in Iraq, the Iraqi constitution was considered to be one of the most progressive in the Middle East: its Article 26 (adopted in 1990) guaranteed "freedom of opinion, publication, meeting, demonstrations and formation of political parties, syndicates, and societies in accordance with the objectives of the Constitution and within the limits of the law."[2] Obviously, neither of those regimes would offer the steadfast support of its political institutions to enforce those provisions, and extremely promising paper guarantees remained just that.

Notwithstanding the American states' swift ratification of an ambitious new Bill of Rights in 1791, the political institutions of the United States have not always stood strong in defense of the First Amendment guarantees of free speech and press in particular. As early as 1798, Congress passed, and President John Adams signed into law, the Alien and Sedition Acts, which, among its other provisions, made it a crime "to speak disparagingly" of the national government or government officials. (Thomas Jefferson pardoned seditious libel defendants upon assuming the presidency in 1801, but only after many had served time in jail.) During World War I, defendants were punished under Congress's Espionage Act for disseminating information opposed to the American war effort. The early years of the Cold War era saw the Truman administration obtain indictments against members of the Communist Party's national board for violating the Smith Act's conspiracy provisions. In each of those instances, Congress and the president were in virtual agreement about these official actions. As is true elsewhere, courts can offer only an occasional bulwark against serious threats to First Amendment freedoms; they are ill suited to fend off repeated violations of free expression when political institutions are unwilling to join the battle.

These truths hold with special force in the context of America's schools. Unlike expression that occurs in public spaces such as parks or street corners, advocacy groups cannot easily monitor threats to students' free expression rights unless students bring their complaints to the public. In the meantime, a confluence of forces has served to increase the threat to student expression in the nation's high schools. These include (1) school administrators motivated to impress their superiors by cracking down on controversial student media; (2) tightening school budgets that have led to diminished support for student media such as school newspapers, radio stations, and the like; and (3) parents who are increasingly reluctant to become pariahs in their local communities by supporting their own children's battles with school officials. Moreover, even if all three of these obstacles could somehow be overcome, there would still be no guarantee that the courts would aggressively protect students' free expression rights in the case of a conflict. In fact, a string of rulings hostile to students' free expression rights beginning in the 1980s and extending up through 2007 counsels for considerable caution in resorting to the courts. A negative court ruling may actually set students' free expression rights backwards.

Given these factors, those interested in protecting the ideal of high schools as a vibrant marketplace of ideas must attempt to look beyond litigation as the primary means of protecting rights. Carefully written state or local policies more effectively pursue the ideal of a marketplace of ideas, if only because they arrive with the intrinsic support of political institutions, rather than as a consequence of legal battles waged against those same institutions. Of course, legislation is not a foolproof means of achieving educational goals. According to the Center for Information and Research on Civic Learning and Engagement (CIRCLE) at the University of Maryland, the relationship between state-level policies and student attitudes toward the First Amendment is weak or somewhat negative.[3] Some especially unpopular policies may be ignored or generate vehement protests. The presence of too many state mandates can prove overwhelming to overworked principals and administrators, causing a negative backlash against even the more reasonable policies.

The Knight Foundation–sponsored surveys of high school students in 2004 and 2006 provide a wake-up call to those interested in preserving the future of free expression rights in American political culture. They document the current lack of appreciation for and understanding of free speech and free press rights among the nation's high school students and, thus, raise serious questions about the vitality of those rights as this generation matures into adulthood. For example, the surveys found that as many as 45 percent of students think the First Amendment goes too far in the rights it guarantees; 30 percent think the press in American has too much freedom; 16 percent think that flag burning as a sign of political dissent should not be allowed; and a bare majority, 54 percent, say that newspapers should be allowed to publish freely without government approval of a news story. Moreover, only 24 percent of high school students say that First Amendment rights are something they personally think about, while the rest admit they either take them for granted (42 percent) or just have not ever thought about them (34 percent).

Despite these rather negative findings, the Knight surveys identified a number of important connections and relationships that reformers ought to account for as they seek to raise the status of the First Amendment among the nation's youth. With respect to curricular offerings, those high school students who take classes with First Amendment or media and society content are more likely to support the exercise of free expression rights. They have better developed opinions about the importance of free expression in this society and are consistently more supportive of pro–First Amendment positions across a variety of topics and situations. Students who take such classes are more likely to feel that the press has an appropriate amount of freedom to do its job effectively. In similar fashion, those who participate in student newspapers are also more likely to support the exercise of free expression rights. In short, this research demonstrates that curricular and extracurricular education matter. When the schools teach students about the First Amendment and free expression rights, students tend to become more supportive of those rights. When students are given an opportunity to practice those rights through participation in a school newspaper, they also develop a greater appreciation for free expression. The important implication here is that curricular and extracurricular reform is likely to have a positive impact on students' orientations toward the First Amendment.

Likewise, the research finds that those who use digital media sources such as blogs and social-networking sites are especially likely to think about and support basic free expression principles. Students who use the Internet to get news and information and those who engage in blogging and other publishing activities enabled by the digital media tend to be more supportive and more appreciative of free expression. Indeed, creating a school environment in which curricular

and extracurricular activities incorporate free expression learning not only promotes student expression rights but instills an appreciation for those rights that
will last a lifetime. This curriculum must account for the new media, which students are rapidly adopting as normal means of communicating in this digital age.

With these facts laid squarely before them, students, educators, school administrators, and reformers came together at several conferences in 2006 and
2007 to take up the challenge of diagnosing the ills facing student expression
in the high schools, then to determine how to treat those ills. Most notably, in
October 2006 the McCormick Tribune Foundation, in collaboration with Ball
State University's J-Ideas program, convened over forty such individuals from
high schools and think tanks around the country in Chicago, Illinois, to consider potential threats to student expression in high schools, such as filters
placed on Internet content on classroom computers and administrative attempts to censor student postings on MySpace.com and other social-networking sites. Less than three months later, the Poynter Institute for Media
Studies in St. Petersburg, Florida, hosted a symposium sponsored by Ball State
University's J-Ideas, featuring forty-five of the nation's top scholastic journalism and civic education leaders. At the January 5, 2007, symposium, a national
alliance was formed to identify public policy initiatives aimed at further em-
bedding the First Amendment in the nation's high schools.

These and other groups have already made significant strides in supporting
First Amendment education and student media across the United States. Ball
State University (acting through J-Ideas since 2003) sponsors residential
workshops that have educated tens of thousands of high school journalists
since 1955. Going a step further, J-Ideas has also created publications and First
Amendment DVDs to assist schools more directly. The Student Press Law
Center, which participated in most of the above conferences and symposia,
has come to the aid of student journalists by giving them free legal advice and
serving as an advocate for their free press and freedom of information rights.

The John S. and James L. Knight Foundation has been a leader in this context as well. In 1950, it established its journalism initiative, which has invested
nearly $300 million to protect and expand press freedoms and encourage
journalism excellence. Since 1986, the foundation has offered a series of major
grants to support journalism fellowship programs at prominent universities.
Working with the American Society of Newspaper Editors, it has disseminated
a variety of lesson plans on journalism-related subjects to high schools; in
conjunction with the Radio and Television News Directors Association and
Foundation, it has also offered a variety of resources for young journalists, including the ever-popular Broadcast in a Box, which includes three books,
three discs, and the RNTDA code of ethics. It also provides information on
best practices in electronic journalism, a video case study on ethical decision
making, and various other teachers' resources.

Just as significant has been the Knight Foundation's efforts to get civics back into schools through the sponsorship of field trips for schools to Philadelphia's Constitution Center, as well as its support of the Newspapers in Education program (which delivers free newspapers to high schools) and the North Carolina Civic Education Consortium, a website that offers resources to help high school students become more involved and civic-minded citizens. Knight and all these organizations have also offered enthusiastic support for national legislation passed in 2004, which requires all secondary schools and colleges to celebrate Constitution Day on or around September 17 of every year (the original Constitution was signed by its drafters in Philadelphia on September 17, 1787). Thanks to the legislation sponsored by Senator Robert Byrd (D-West Virginia), school administrators must start grappling with this mandate, considering potential ways to commemorate the event. At a minimum, this legislation has raised many students' awareness of the First Amendment and the Bill of Rights as a whole.

Even more sweeping policy initiatives and proposals are laid out below, each offering some promise of balancing the interests of free and unfettered student expression with the continuous demands for order and respect for the rights of others in the nation's high schools.

Increasing the Availability of Student Media Outlets in the Schools

One of the maladies that afflict high schools today was identified in chapter 2. Participation in school newspapers and other forms of student media tend to increase appreciation for free expression rights among the current generation of high school students. Thus, high schools should be increasing the opportunities available to their students to engage in student media, whether in the form of newspapers, magazines, broadcast media, or digital media. Unfortunately, some of the trends identified in the Future of the First Amendment surveys appear to be moving in the opposite direction. A substantial percentage (40 percent) of the schools that do not currently offer student newspapers say they eliminated their newspapers in the five years prior to the 2004 survey. Urban and lower-income schools have been especially hard hit. Although some of the slack has been picked up by less expensive Internet publications, they cannot fully substitute for the educational aspects of writing, editing, publishing, and distributing a student newspaper or print publication to the community at large.

Adding a Stronger Civics Component to the High School Curriculum

According to Molly McCloskey, director of Constituent Partnerships, a national association concerned with curriculum development in high schools, there is a natural connection established among curriculum development supervisors, civics education advocates, and student journalists as a whole. As high school students begin to assume their civic duties and responsibilities, they become more likely to ask questions regarding controversial issues in their own high schools and elsewhere. A student's willingness to publish what he or she knows or thinks about to the community at large, whether through formally sanctioned student media outlets or private blogs and social-networking sites, offers him or her the opportunity to take on the role of reporter, as well as editor and publisher of his or her own material. A well-grounded education in civics can provide students with all the tools necessary to better understand the nature of the publishing enterprise and how it can most effectively serve democracy.

In chapter 2 we documented the degree to which civic education in America today includes education about the First Amendment, free expression rights, and the role of media in society. Some progress was noted between 2004 and 2006, as the clear majority of students (72 percent) by 2006 confirmed that they had indeed taken classes that dealt with the First Amendment; yet, when it comes to civics courses that discuss the role of media in society, a smaller percentage (62 percent) in 2006 indicated that they had taken such classes. Chapter 3 spelled out in clear terms the relationship that exists between civics course work and students' attitudes about First Amendment rights. Students who have taken classes with First Amendment content or classes that discuss the role of the media in society are more likely to express opinions about the First Amendment in general. Moreover, the opinions they express are more likely to be favorable. What's the bottom line? Students who take civics courses with First Amendment or media components are more likely to form opinions and attitudes about the First Amendment. This in turn puts in place a crucial foundation within each high school community, as students can more effectively exercise their responsibilities as journalists and disseminators of information.

Unfortunately, while civics technically remains part of the required curriculum in many school districts across the country, the vast majority of schools are not currently required to test a student's knowledge in this area. Consequently, subjects heavily tested under federal No Child Left Behind legislation predominate in most elementary, middle, and high school curricula. There have been some important breakthroughs in this regard. Beginning in 2008 and 2009, the state of Washington will require its school districts to measure students' knowledge in civics either with a state-approved, classroom-based civics assessment or by some other method. However, the state of Washington remains unique in this regard. In fact, resistance to such initiatives may actually be increasing, as school districts already burdened by No Child Left Behind legislation are understandably reluctant to dump yet another load of tests on their principals' doorsteps.

Adding a Media Literacy Component to the High School Curriculum

In an era when student journalists can write and disseminate information on virtually any subject imaginable through blogs, social-networking sites, and other Internet sources, reformers have increasingly turned their attention to searching for means of helping students better understand the nature of the power they actually wield. At least one defense against the threat of censorship is evidence that student journalists take seriously their responsibilities as members of the media by taking classes in media literacy. Schools should be offering instruction in the informed and responsible use of the digital media because those who access blogs, social-networking sites, and other digital media, as well as those who post messages and publish through those digital media forms, are more likely to express appreciation for free expression rights in general. In sum, training students to navigate the digital media landscape represents one of the most effective means available of enhancing tolerance for the First Amendment among this latest generation of Americans.

By learning how to evaluate carefully what they read and see in the traditional media and the online world, students can effectively separate valuable from relatively useless information. Some of the skills and information considered especially crucial to media literacy in the twenty-first century are the following:

- interpreting the validity of URLs and Web addresses
- searching for and choosing the websites most suitable for research
- evaluating various forms of online advertising
- evaluating the content of websites for obvious signs of bias
- spotting bogus or fraudulent websites
- using e-mail and chat rooms responsibly

Naturally, courses in journalism skills offer one potential source of such media literacy skills. A comprehensive course that trains students to be effective journalists would necessarily have to offer them help in sifting through different types of evidence on the Internet and elsewhere. Unfortunately, chapter 2 offered the finding that barely a quarter of high school students in 2006 indicated they had taken classes that dealt primarily with journalism skills. A course that merely touches on journalism skills in just one component is not likely to include a thorough and comprehensive education in any aspect of journalism, including these media literacy skills. Educational reformers facing tightened budgets see this as one of the greatest challenges they face, albeit one with an immense potential payoff for democracy.

Passing Legislation to Support Student Free Press Rights

In chapter 1 we offered a profile of national adult attitudes about the First Amendment that was not always encouraging to free speech advocates. Confirming a trend that dates back to the 1960s, while free expression rights in general tend to fare well in the court of public opinion, more concrete and controversial situations invite a different reaction: the public has been far less willing to afford freedom to groups such as Communist sympathizers, Nazis, and homosexuals, for example. In more recent State of the First Amendment surveys of the adult population conducted for the Freedom Forum, approximately nine in ten adults agree with the statement that people should be allowed to express their opinion, whatever that opinion might be. Yet, at the same time, only a bare majority (51 percent) thinks musicians should be allowed to sing songs with lyrics that might be offensive, just 41 percent think people should be allowed to display art whose context might be offensive to some, and a mere 45 percent think people should be allowed to publish sexually explicit material in magazines. Support for the rights of public school students to engage in controversial speech is even lower. For example, only 27 percent think that public school students should be allowed to wear a T-shirt with a message that is offensive to some.

Given the reluctance of so many in the public to support specific forms of free expression, legislation that offers expanded protection to student journalists tends to generate little sustained support from representatives in state legislatures. To date, only six states (Arkansas, California, Colorado, Iowa, Kansas, and Massachusetts) have passed legislation giving enhanced free press guarantees to students. Moreover, the most recent of those states to do so, Arkansas, accomplished the feat over a decade ago, in 1995.

The state of Washington has also had its share of frustrations. In March 2007, the Washington State House of Representatives passed a bill to protect high school students and college students from censorship and prior review by school administrators. Sponsored by State Representative Dave Upthegrove from suburban Seattle, this legislation would have applied to student-run, student-edited newspapers; no journalism advisor could be fired or punished for refusing to suppress student newspapers. Further, because expression by students cannot rightfully be considered a statement of school policy, the Washington bill would also have ensured that school officials also couldn't be sued for student content under the bill. Unfortunately, the Washington State Senate's Judiciary Committee first removed high schools from the bill, then rejected it outright.

Despite these frustrations, there are signs of a new political trend in favor of student press freedoms. One of the original six states to pass legislation,

California, recently passed new legislation to ensure that the collegiate student press would be protected from censorship as well. Oregon's legislature considered student free expression legislation in 2001; the Oregon bill would have applied free press protections to high school and college media. Six years later, Oregon's own student free press bill (modeled after the original Washington State House bill) passed that state's House and Senate in 2007. Vermont and Michigan have also launched efforts to pass similar student free press legislation. In early 2007, the Vermont legislature was considering a bill to counteract the decision in *Hazelwood v. Kuhlmeier* and protect students' free expression rights in school-sponsored publications, so long as the content is not "obscene, libelous, defamatory or invades someone's privacy." Also in 2007, Michigan State Senator Michael Switalski launched a second attempt to protect Michigan's K-12 students from censorship and prior review (his first attempt was killed in committee in early 2005).

Are these student free press policies effective? Certainly, some schools may ignore the legislation, and the lack of enforceability is always a concern. However, the vast majority of student journalists will act responsibly and abide by appropriate school policies, regardless of the legal rules and restrictions. Still, if the greatest threat to student expression comes from school administrators who may choose to clamp down on controversial publications out of fear of lawsuits and the complaints of parents, legislation that in effect shields school administrators from these pressures can only be beneficial. They also offer a symbolic show of support for school administrators that cannot easily be ignored.

Educating Principals and Teachers about the First Amendment

Surveys conducted by the John S. and James L. Knight Foundation in 2004 and 2006 did not limit themselves to the student population: teachers and administrators were also surveyed about their knowledge of and attitudes toward the First Amendment. In 2004, just 33 percent of the principals surveyed felt it was "very important" that students learn journalism skills; more than half thought their schools offered "about the right amount" of student media clubs and "the right amount" of courses on journalism. Teachers on the front lines were not much more supportive; in 2004, only 35 percent of teachers surveyed thought it was very important that all students learn journalism skills. Clearly, tightened budgets are a significant problem, but they are not the only one: many of these same teachers and principals are more supportive of extracurricular activities in general than they are of student media and journalism activities in particular.

Clearly, reorienting teachers' and principals' attitudes represents a fundamental opportunity for educational reformers. If those two groups are apathetic about the need for journalism education, they are not likely to be the foremost advocates of student media. Moreover, educators enjoy a wide amount of discretion in the way they choose to exercise their professional judgment in overseeing journalism programs and student media outlets. If their decisions are based on "sound educational and pedagogical principles," the educational mission can be most effectively served. Of course, administrator and faculty education programs will only succeed if they grapple realistically with the dilemmas facing those individuals. Simply advocating free expression to these groups could prove counterproductive in the short run.

* * * * * *

Looking ahead, there may be other ways to put the First Amendment first in the nation's high schools that are less immediate in their impact but may have significant effects over the long haul. For example, more and more schools are actively considering adopting mission statements that prominently feature the role of schools in fulfilling civic ideals through civic education. Educational reformers hope that formally articulating the importance of student press freedoms and education about them will set a tone in favor of free expression for students, teachers, and principals alike. A fourth group, the parents of high school students, offers yet another possibility for reform. If parents are educated about the importance of free expression rights in the high schools and are involved in student journalism activities, everyone wins. Administrators who may be overly concerned with impressing superintendents and other superiors are still responsible to parents and must take their demands into account. To the extent that parents are educated in and sophisticated about these subjects, they can offer an alternative viewpoint to weigh against potentially rash decisions to censor or otherwise restrict student expression.

These and other proposals are offered as part of a far-ranging and important conversation currently taking place among student administrators, reformers, academics, and even some legislators concerning the future of student press freedoms. In the digital age, these freedoms manifest themselves in paper and electronic form—through newspapers, cable television outlets, social-networking sites, and countless other means—as crafted by aspiring young journalists as well as those with no aspirations at all beyond updating their blogs on MySpace.com. Of course, as we have argued in these pages, student press freedoms cannot be considered in isolation; they serve as a foundation for the next generation of citizens' knowledge of and appreciation for their own First Amendment rights. Today's generation of high school students is only now becoming aware of its important civic responsibilities. Society must embrace their methods of communication and defend their freedoms. The stakes are too great to wait much longer.

Notes

1. Article 50 of the Constitution of the Union of Soviet Socialist Republics (USSR) (1977) held in full, "In accordance with the interest of the people and in order to strengthen and develop the socialist system, citizens of the USSR are guaranteed freedom of speech, of the press, and of assembly, meetings, street processions and demonstrations. Exercise of these political freedoms is ensured by putting public buildings, streets and squares at the disposal of the working people and their organizations, by broad dissemination of information, and by the opportunity to use the press, television and radio."

2. The text of the 1990 Iraq constitution was published as part of the International Constitutional Law Project at the University of Wuerzberg in Wuerzberg, Germany. (See "Interim Constitution of Iraq (1990)," Iraq Foundation, www.iraqfoundation .org/projects/constitution/local_iraq1990.pdf (accessed 1 March 2008).

3. Since 2001, CIRCLE, based at the University of Maryland's School of Public Policy, has conducted, collected, and funded research on the civic engagement and education and the political participation of young Americans. Funded by the Pew Charitable Trusts and Carnegie Corporation of New York, CIRCLE's website can be found at www.civicyouth.org (accessed January 26, 2008).

Appendix A

Knight Future of the First Amendment 2004 and 2006 Student and Faculty Questionnaires

Knight FOFA High School Student Survey, 2004 and 2006

1. What grade are you currently in?

	2004	2006
Below 9th	2%	0%
9th	29%	30%
10th	27%	27%
11th	23%	24%
12th	19%	18%

2. How interested are you in following news and current events in general?

	2006
Extremely interested	4%
Very interested	17%
Somewhat interested	69%
Not interested at all	10%

3. There are many reasons why people say they don't pay attention to the news. Please CIRCLE whether or not each of the following is a reason why you may not pay attention to the news.

	2006
I'm too busy	67%
I get my news from friends or family	67%

The news doesn't affect me personally	28%
The news is not presented in an interesting way	40%
I can't understand it	12%
Other reasons: _____	8%

4. Do you currently have access to the Internet?

	2006
At home	87%
At school	97%

5. Short for "Web logs," "blogs" are defined as online journals in which people post diary entries about their personal experiences and opinions to be read online by others. Examples of blog collections include Myspace.com and Facebook.com. How often, if at all, do you get news and information from blogs?

	2006
Every day	9%
Several times a week	11%
About once a week	12%
Less than once a week	16%
Never	52%

6. How often, if at all, do you get news and information from online or Internet sources in general? (If you answer NEVER, skip to page 2.)

	2006
Every day	11%
Several times a week	20%
About once a week	20%
Less than once a week	20%
Never	29%

7a. How often, if at all, do you get news and information from the following sources: the news pages of Internet service providers such as Google news, Microsoft news, AOL news, or Yahoo! news?

	2006
Every day	18%
Several times a week	25%
About once a week	23%
Less than once a week	22%
Never	12%

7b. How often, if at all, do you get news and information from the following sources: network TV news websites such as CNN.com, ABCNews.com, or MSNBC.com?

	2006
Every day	9%
Several times a week	17%
About once a week	19%
Less than once a week	27%
Never	28%

7c. How often, if at all, do you get news and information from the following sources: the websites of major national newspapers such as USAToday .com, NewYorkTimes.com, or the *Wall Street Journal* online?

	2006
Every day	3%
Several times a week	6%
About once a week	12%
Less than once a week	26%
Never	53%

7d. How often, if at all, do you get news and information from the following sources: the websites of your local newspaper or TV stations?

	2006
Every day	7%
Several times a week	12%
About once a week	15%
Less than once a week	26%
Never	40%

8. How often, if at all, do you get news and information from entertainment programs that feature some discussion of current events, such as the *Daily Show*, the *Colbert Report*, and *South Park*?

	2006
Every day	8%
Several times a week	18%
About once a week	20%
Less than once a week	21%
Never	33%

9a. Which of these media sources do you consider the best overall source of news?

	2006
Newspapers	23%
Magazines	5%
Radio stations	9%
Television stations	45%
Blogs	1%
Internet publications other than blogs	10%
Entertainment programs featuring current events	7%

9b. Which of these media sources do you consider the most accurate?

	2006
Newspapers	35%
Magazines	3%
Radio stations	6%
Television stations	44%
Blogs	1%
Internet publications other than blogs	9%
Entertainment programs featuring current events	3%

9c. Which of these media sources do you consider the easiest to use?

	2006
Newspapers	12%
Magazines	3%
Radio stations	11%
Television stations	43%
Blogs	2%
Internet publications other than blogs	21%
Entertainment programs featuring current events	7%

10. How much do you trust journalists to tell the truth? Do you believe they tell the truth . . .

	2004	2006
All of the time	4%	4%
Some of the time	58%	59%
Little of the time	23%	23%
Not at all	9%	6%
Don't know	6%	8%

11. Do you feel that the emergence of the Internet has made journalism better or worse or hasn't made much of a difference?

	2006
Better	30%
Worse	20%
Not much difference	50%

12a. Now, thinking about what you *do* online, how often, if at all, do you use the Internet, the World Wide Web, or an online service to send or receive e-mails to select individuals or groups of individuals?

	2006
Every day	30%
Several times a week	26%
About once a week	15%
Less than once a week	14%
Never	15%

12b. Now, thinking about what you *do* online, how often, if at all, do you use the Internet, the World Wide Web, or an online service to participate in online discussions or chat groups?

	2006
Every day	18%
Several times a week	16%
About once a week	10%
Less than once a week	16%
Never	41%

12c. Now, thinking about what you *do* online, how often, if at all, do you use the Internet, the World Wide Web, or an online service to post messages or opinions to online columns or blogs that may be read by the general public?

	2006
Every day	10%
Several times a week	11%
About once a week	11%
Less than once a week	17%
Never	51%

13a. Have you ever taken classes in high school that dealt with the First Amendment to the U.S. Constitution?

	2004	2006
Yes	58%	72%
No	42%	28%

13b. Have you ever taken classes in high school that discuss the role of media in society?

	2004	2006
Yes	52%	62%
No	48%	38%

13c. Have you ever taken classes in high school that dealt primarily with journalism skills?

	2004	2006
Yes	21%	26%
No	79%	74%

13d. Have you ever taken a class in high school where the teacher required as a class assignment that you read a newspaper or watch television news?

	2004	2006
Yes	75%	81%
No	25%	19%

14. Please indicate whether or not you have been involved in any of the following activities at your high school. (Check all that apply.)

	2004	2006
Student newspaper	8%	10%
Student magazine with a news component (does not include literary magazines or yearbooks)	4%	2%
Student-run radio station with a news component	4%	2%
Student-run television station with a news component	5%	5%
Student Internet or World Wide Web publication with a news component	5%	5%
Any other form of student media with a news component	5%	4%

15. The First Amendment became part of the U.S. Constitution more than two hundred years ago. This is what it says: "Congress shall make no law respecting an establishment of religion or prohibiting the free exercise thereof, or abridging the freedom of speech or of the press, or the right of the people peaceably to assemble, and to petition the government for a redress of grievances."

Based on your own feelings about the First Amendment, please tell me whether you agree or disagree with the following statement: "The First Amendment goes too far in the rights it guarantees."

	2004	2006
Strongly agree	12%	18%
Mildly agree	23%	27%
Mildly disagree	19%	16%
Strongly disagree	25%	21%
Don't know	21%	19%

16. Overall, do you think the press in America has too much freedom to do what it wants, too little freedom to do what it wants, or is the amount of freedom the press has about right?

	2004	2006
Too much freedom	32%	30%
Too little freedom	10%	11%
About right	37%	41%
Don't know	21%	18%

17a. People should be allowed to express unpopular opinions.

	2004	2006
Strongly agree	51%	52%
Mildly agree	32%	33%
Mildly disagree	5%	5%
Strongly disagree	2%	2%
Don't know	10%	8%

17b. People should be allowed to burn or deface the American flag as a political statement.

	2004	2006
Strongly agree	8%	7%
Mildly agree	8%	9%
Mildly disagree	11%	12%
Strongly disagree	63%	64%
Don't know	10%	8%

17c. Musicians should be allowed to sing songs with lyrics that others might find offensive.

	2004	2006
Strongly agree	40%	37%
Mildly agree	30%	32%
Mildly disagree	14%	16%
Strongly disagree	7%	7%
Don't know	9%	8%

17d. Newspapers should be allowed to publish freely without government approval of a story.

	2004	2006
Strongly agree	24%	26%
Mildly agree	27%	28%
Mildly disagree	22%	23%
Strongly disagree	14%	13%
Don't know	13%	10%

17e. High school students should be allowed to report controversial issues in their student newspapers without the approval of school authorities.

	2004	2006
Strongly agree	30%	34%
Mildly agree	28%	30%
Mildly disagree	18%	17%
Strongly disagree	11%	8%
Don't know	13%	11%

18. Do you agree or disagree with the following statement: "Americans don't appreciate First Amendment freedoms the way they ought to"?

	2004	2006
Strongly agree	17%	15%
Mildly agree	33%	38%
Mildly disagree	18%	17%
Strongly disagree	9%	7%
Don't know	23%	23%

19. Are the rights guaranteed by the First Amendment something you personally think about, or are they something you take for granted?

	2004	2006
Personally think about	27%	24%
Take for granted	36%	42%
Don't know	37%	34%

20. Are you male or female?

	2004	2006
Male	50%	50%
Female	50%	50%

21. Are you Spanish/Hispanic/Latino?

	2004	2006
Yes	15%	12%
No	85%	88%

22. What is your race?

	2004	2006
White/Caucasian	68%	73%
Black/African American	14%	11%
American Indian/Alaska Native	2%	1%
Asian	4%	3%
Some other race	12%	12%

23. Thinking about your family's current financial situation, do you consider yourself to be rich, upper income, middle income, lower income, or poor?

	2004	2006
Rich	5%	4%
Upper income	23%	24%
Middle income	59%	61%
Lower income	10%	9%
Poor	4%	2%

24. What is your approximate overall high school grade point average?

	2004	2006
0.0–2.0 (or 0–75)	7%	6%
2.1–3.0 (or 76–85)	31%	31%
3.1–3.5 (or 86–90)	31%	32%
3.6–4.0 (or 91–95)	22%	23%
Over 4.0 (over 95)	9%	8%

25. Which of the following grades is closest to your current overall grade point average?

	2004	2006
A	28%	30%
B	42%	45%
C	23%	21%
D	4%	3%
F	2%	1%

26. Which of the following best describes you?

	2004	2006
I was born a U.S. citizen	90%	94%
I was born in another country, but became a U.S. citizen	5%	3%
I was born in another country, and I am not a U.S. citizen	5%	3%

27. Do you have any additional comments?

Knight FOFA High School Faculty Survey, 2004 and 2006

1. What subject or subjects do you currently teach? (Please check all that apply.)

	2004	2006
Art/music/drama	8%	8%
English	21%	18%
Foreign language (e.g., Spanish, French)	8%	8%
History	11%	8%
Journalism	2%	2%
Math (algebra/calculus/geometry)	17%	14%
Physical education	6%	6%
Physical sciences (e.g., biology/ chemistry/physics)	14%	12%
Psychology	2%	1%
Social studies	12%	12%
Special education	9%	10%
Other	26%	25%

2. During the past year, have you taught any classes that dealt primarily with journalism skills?

	2004	2006
Yes	7%	8%
No	93%	92%

3. During the past year, have you taught any classes that deal with the First Amendment?

	2004	2006
Yes	24%	29%
No	76%	71%

4. During the past year, have you taught any classes that discuss the role of media in society?

	2004	2006
Yes	42%	44%
No	58%	56%

5. During the past year, have you required as an assignment that your students read a newspaper or watch the television news, and if so, how often were they required to do so?

	2004	2006
Never	44%	45%
Once per year	12%	11%
On a quarterly basis	17%	16%

On a monthly basis	12%	11%
On a weekly basis	14%	17%

6. Do you currently serve as faculty advisor to any of the following clubs or activities? (Please check all that apply, or check NONE.)

	2004	2006
Student newspaper	4%	2%
Student magazine (category does *not* include student literary magazines or yearbooks)	1%	0%
Student-run radio station with a news component	0%	0%
Student-run television station with a news component	1%	1%
Student Internet or World Wide Web publication with a news component	2%	1%
Any other form of student media with a news component _____	5%	2%

7. How important do you feel it is that ALL students participate in some extracurricular activities or clubs?

	2004	2006
Very important	73%	69%
Somewhat important	24%	28%
Not too important	2%	2%
Not important at all	1%	0%
Don't know	0%	1%

8. How important do you feel it is that ALL students learn some journalism skills?

	2004	2006
Very important	35%	31%
Somewhat important	52%	55%
Not too important	10%	11%
Not important at all	1%	1%
Don't know	1%	3%

9. How important do you feel it is that ALL students learn to effectively use the Internet or World Wide Web to collect news or information?

	2006
Very important	85%
Somewhat important	14%
Not too important	1%

| Not important at all | 0% |
| Don't know | 0% |

10. During the past year, how often did you require as part of an assignment that your students do research using the World Wide Web or the Internet?

	2006
Never	14%
Once per year	14%
On a quarterly basis	34%
On a monthly basis	26%
On a weekly basis	12%

11. During the past year, how often did you require as part of an assignment that your students communicate with each other by e-mail, chat group, or some other form of online discussion?

	2006
Never	86%
Once per year	3%
On a quarterly basis	4%
On a monthly basis	5%
On a weekly basis	2%

12. Short for "Web logs," "blogs" are defined as online journals in which people post diary entries about their personal experiences and opinions to be read online by others. How often, if at all, do you get news and information from blogs?

	2006
Every day	2%
Several times a week	3%
About once a week	4%
Less than once a week	14%
Never	72%
Don't know	5%

Now, thinking about all the different media sources available to students . . .

13. Which of these media sources do you consider the best overall source of news?
(Please check only one.)

	2006
Newspapers	48%
Magazines	3%
Radio stations	5%

Television stations	28%
Blogs	1%
Internet publications other than blogs	15%
Entertainment programs featuring current events	1%

14. How much do you trust journalists to tell the truth? Do you believe they tell the truth . . .

	2004	2006
All of the time	4%	5%
Some of the time	79%	84%
Little of the time	13%	7%
Not at all	2%	2%
Don't know	2%	2%

15. The First Amendment became part of the U.S. Constitution more than two hundred years ago. This is what it says: "Congress shall make no law respecting an establishment of religion or prohibiting the free exercise thereof, or abridging the freedom of speech or of the press, or the right of the people peaceably to assemble, and to petition the government for a redress of grievances."

    Based on your own feelings about the First Amendment, please tell me whether you strongly agree, mildly agree, mildly disagree, or strongly disagree with the following statement: "The First Amendment goes too far in the rights it guarantees."

	2004	2006
Strongly agree	9%	12%
Mildly agree	20%	21%
Mildly disagree	16%	12%
Strongly disagree	50%	50%
Don't know	5%	5%

16. Overall, how would you rate the job that the American educational system does in teaching students about First Amendment freedoms?

	2004	2006
Excellent	7%	6%
Good	46%	42%
Fair	29%	33%
Poor	7%	9%
Don't know	11%	10%

17. Overall, do you think the press in America has too much freedom to do what it wants, too little freedom to do what it wants, or is the amount of freedom the press has about right?

	2004	2006
Too much freedom	38%	29%
Too little freedom	8%	10%
About right	49%	55%
Don't know	6%	6%

18a. People should be allowed to express unpopular opinions.

	2004	2006
Strongly agree	72%	75%
Mildly agree	25%	21%
Mildly disagree	2%	3%
Strongly disagree	1%	1%
Don't know	1%	0%

18b. People should be allowed to burn or deface the American flag as a political statement.

	2004	2006
Strongly agree	15%	16%
Mildly agree	13%	13%
Mildly disagree	11%	11%
Strongly disagree	59%	58%
Don't know	2%	2%

18c. Musicians should be allowed to sing songs with lyrics that others might find offensive.

	2004	2006
Strongly agree	28%	35%
Mildly agree	30%	29%
Mildly disagree	19%	19%
Strongly disagree	21%	15%
Don't know	2%	2%

18d. Newspapers should be allowed to publish freely without government approval of a story.

	2004	2006
Strongly agree	53%	57%
Mildly agree	27%	22%
Mildly disagree	12%	13%
Strongly disagree	6%	7%
Don't know	2%	1%

18e. High school students should be allowed to report controversial issues in their student newspapers without the approval of school authorities.

	2004	2006
Strongly agree	13%	13%
Mildly agree	26%	27%
Mildly disagree	27%	28%
Strongly disagree	33%	31%
Don't know	1%	1%

19. Do you agree or disagree with the following statement: "Americans don't appreciate First Amendment freedoms the way they ought to"?

	2004	2006
Strongly agree	30%	32%
Mildly agree	43%	47%
Mildly disagree	14%	12%
Strongly disagree	5%	4%
Don't know	7%	5%

20. Are the rights guaranteed by the First Amendment something you personally think about, or are they something you take for granted?

	2004	2006
Personally think about	50%	49%
Take for granted	46%	47%
Don't know	4%	4%

21. What about most people in the United States—do you think the rights guaranteed by the First Amendment are something people specifically think about, or are they something they take for granted?

	2004	2006
Personally think about	7%	5%
Take for granted	86%	89%
Don't know	7%	6%

Finally, please answer the following questions for classification purposes only.
22. What is the highest level of education that you have attained?

	2004	2006
High school diploma	1%	1%
Bachelor's	41%	41%
Master's	52%	53%

ABD (all but dissertation)	3%	3%
Doctorate	1%	2%
Postdoctorate	0%	0%
Don't know	2%	0%

23. Have you ever received any formal instruction in the First Amendment?

	2004	2006
Yes	51%	57%
No	49%	43%

24. IF YES, would that have been before high school, during high school, and/or after high school? (Check all that apply.)

	2004	2006
Before high school	21%	13%
During high school	75%	43%
After high school	54%	35%
Don't know	1%	0%

25. Age?

	2004	2006
18–28	11%	14%
29–39	27%	27%
40–50	27%	28%
51–61	32%	29%
62–72	3%	2%
73+	0%	0%

26. Are you male or female?

	2004	2006
Male	42%	42%
Female	58%	58%

27. Are you Spanish/Hispanic/Latino?

	2004	2006
Yes	3%	6%
No	97%	94%

28. What is your race?

	2004	2006
White/Caucasian	92%	94%
Black/African American	4%	3%
American Indian/Alaska Native	0%	0%
Asian	1%	0%
Some other race	2%	3%

Appendix B

Future of the First Amendment
Survey Sampling Methodology

Sample Designs for 2004 and 2006 FOFA Surveys

THE JOHN S. AND JAMES L. KNIGHT FOUNDATION commissioned Dr. David Yalof and Dr. Ken Dautrich at the University of Connecticut to conduct the 2004 and 2006 surveys of high school students, teachers, and principals across the country.

Sampling for the 2004 survey included a multistage cluster sample. The initial stage of the sampling included drawing a random sample of 544 high school buildings from across the fifty states. Principals were contacted from these schools and asked for their school's cooperation. A total of 327 of the schools cooperated. For each of these 327 schools, teachers and students took self-administered surveys. Students anonymously answered the survey during homeroom period. Teachers answered the survey at a convenient time during the school day. Also, the 327 principals were asked to answer a third survey. The sample demographics of the schools were measured against Patterson's American Education high school database demographics to ensure the representativeness of the school samples. The initial sample of 544 schools was drawn from Educational Directories of Schaumberg, Illinois, which is a comprehensive, single-source database of both public and private high schools in the United States.

The sample of schools was stratified to proportionately represent public and nonpublic schools of different sizes. In the first stage of the design, schools were selected with equal probabilities of selection. In the second stage, the survey was designed to interview all faculty, students, and principals at the schools.

Data collection for the 2004 study was conducted in March through May of 2004. A total of 112,003 students, 7,889 teachers, and 3,008 principals returned completed surveys.

For the 2006 FOFA survey, a random sample of 45 schools from the initial 544 schools was selected. Principals were contacted and asked for their school's participation. Thirty-seven schools cooperated. Surveys were administered to all students and teachers in these thirty-seven schools. A total of 14,498 students and 882 teachers completed surveys. Data collection for the 2006 survey was conducted from March through May of 2006.

Appendix C

Full Multivariate Model Results

Table C.1
Dependent Variable: "Extremely" or "Very" Interested in
Following the News and Current Events (Q2). Probit Results.

Curriculum and Courses	
Taken class in high school:	(1)
That dealt with the First Amendment and U.S. Constitution	0.068*
	(0.032)
That dealt with the role of media in society	0.106***
	(0.028)
That dealt primarily with journalism skills	0.033
	(0.030)
Where teacher required reading of newspaper or watching of television news	0.084*
	(0.034)
Extracurricular Activities with News Content	
Student newspaper	0.238***
	(0.043)
Student magazine	0.068
	(0.084)
Student radio	−0.158
	(0.099)

(continued)

Table C.1 *(continued)*

Student television station	0.065
	(0.057)
Student Internet publication	0.101
	(0.065)
Other student news activity	0.066
	(0.063)
Internet Use and News Consumption	
Use Internet frequently for news	0.752***
	(0.035)
Use Internet infrequently for news	0.234***
	(0.033)
Use blogs frequently for news	−0.117**
	(0.038)
Use blogs infrequently for news	−0.078*
	(0.031)
Use chat rooms frequently	−0.138***
	(0.032)
Use chat rooms infrequently	−0.022
	(0.032)
Blog frequently	0.084*
	(0.038)
Blog infrequently	0.056
	(0.032)
Demographics and Other Characteristics	
Female	−0.191***
	(0.026)
Hispanic	0.255***
	(0.041)
African American	0.110*
	(0.043)
Asian American	−0.167*
	(0.077)
Other race/ethnicity	0.032
	(0.060)
U.S. citizen	−0.157*
	(0.067)
Economic class—upper income	0.129*
	(0.065)
Economic class—middle income	0.131***
	(0.029)

Table C.1 *(continued)*

Economic class—lower income	0.015
	(0.046)
Economic class—poor	−0.002
	(0.086)
Economic class—missing	0.060
	(0.092)
Internet access at home	−0.083*
	(0.040)
Internet access at school	−0.003
	(0.050)
Secular private school	0.279
	(0.146)
Religious private school	0.050
	(0.042)
Self-reported GPA—B	−0.174***
	(0.029)
Self-reported GPA—C	−0.391***
	(0.038)
Self-reported GPA—D	−0.536***
	(0.091)
Self-reported GPA—F	−0.198
	(0.118)
Self-reported GPA missing	1.016***
	(0.186)
10th grader	0.065
	(0.035)
11th grader	0.122***
	(0.036)
12th grader	0.228***
	(0.039)
Constant	−1.034***
	(0.097)
Sample size	14,414

Source: Author's tabulations from FOFA 2006.

Note: Robust standard errors are in parentheses; all standard errors have been adjusted for heteroscedasticity: * significant at 10 percent; ** significant at 5 percent; *** significant at 1 percent.

Table C.2
Dependent Variable: Does the First Amendment Go Too Far in the Rights It Guarantees (Q15)? Base Group: Agree. Multinomial Logit Results.

	Disagree	No Opinion
Curriculum and Courses		
Taken class in high school:	(1)	(2)
That dealt with the First Amendment and U.S. Constitution	0.030	−0.333***
	(0.049)	(0.056)
That dealt with the role of media in society	0.080	−0.210***
	(0.044)	(0.052)
That dealt primarily with journalism skills	−0.358***	0.034
	(0.048)	(0.057)
Where teacher required reading of newspaper or watching of television news	0.016	−0.230***
	(0.053)	(0.058)
Extracurricular Activities with News Content		
Student newspaper	0.300***	−0.106
	(0.070)	(0.097)
Student magazine	−0.189	−0.355
	(0.147)	(0.197)
Student radio	−0.281	−0.181
	(0.169)	(0.198)
Student television station	0.087	0.111
	(0.095)	(0.121)
Student Internet publication	−0.071	−0.101
	(0.109)	(0.149)
Other student news activity	−0.186	−0.292
	(0.108)	(0.151)
Internet Use and News Consumption		
Use Internet frequently for news	0.123*	−0.724***
	(0.054)	(0.069)
Use Internet infrequently for news	0.058	−0.323***
	(0.049)	(0.055)
Use blogs frequently for news	−0.207***	−0.181*
	(0.058)	(0.075)
Use blogs infrequently for news	−0.111*	−0.194**
	(0.048)	(0.060)

Table C.2 *(continued)*

	Disagree	No Opinion
Use chat rooms frequently	−0.137**	−0.105
	(0.050)	(0.061)
Use chat rooms infrequently	0.056	−0.157*
	(0.051)	(0.063)
Blog frequently	0.069	−0.190*
	(0.059)	(0.075)
Blog infrequently	0.129**	−0.040
	(0.050)	(0.062)
Demographics and Other Characteristics		
Female	−0.097*	0.335***
	(0.040)	(0.049)
Hispanic	−0.215***	−0.335***
	(0.065)	(0.081)
African American	−0.448***	−0.183*
	(0.071)	(0.077)
Asian American	−0.421***	0.003
	(0.118)	(0.147)
Other race/ethnicity	−0.206*	0.027
	(0.094)	(0.106)
U.S. citizen	0.212	0.014
	(0.113)	(0.128)
Economic class—upper income	−0.249*	0.217
	(0.111)	(0.122)
Economic class—middle income	0.013	−0.139*
	(0.046)	(0.061)
Economic class—lower income	0.140	0.109
	(0.072)	(0.084)
Economic class—poor	0.289*	0.534***
	(0.141)	(0.144)
Economic class—missing	−0.058	0.123
	(0.150)	(0.169)
Internet access at home	0.026	0.134
	(0.064)	(0.071)
Internet access at school	0.070	−0.008
	(0.081)	(0.087)
Secular private school	−0.616*	0.182
	(0.294)	(0.240)

(continued)

Table C.2 *(continued)*

	Disagree	No Opinion
Religious private school	0.101	−0.067
	(0.065)	(0.091)
Self-reported GPA—B	−0.549***	0.100
	(0.045)	(0.062)
Self-reported GPA—C	−0.846***	0.349***
	(0.059)	(0.071)
Self-reported GPA—D	−0.555***	0.718***
	(0.131)	(0.130)
Self-reported GPA—F	−0.080	0.956***
	(0.204)	(0.202)
Self-reported GPA missing	1.643***	−1.702***
	(0.297)	(0.320)
10th grader	0.146**	−0.040
	(0.053)	(0.061)
11th grader	0.349***	−0.047
	(0.056)	(0.068)
12th grader	0.602***	0.042
	(0.062)	(0.079)
Constant	−0.236	−0.229
	(0.160)	(0.181)
Sample size		14,405

Source: Author's tabulations from FOFA 2006.

Note: Robust standard errors are in parentheses; all standard errors have been adjusted for heteroscedasticity: * significant at 10 percent; ** significant at 5 percent; *** significant at 1 percent.

Table C.3
Do You Think the Press in America Has Too Much Freedom (Q16)?
Base Group: Too Much Freedom. Multinomial Logit Results.

	Too Little Freedom	About Right	Don't Know
Curriculum and Courses *Taken class in high school:*	(1)	(2)	(3)
That dealt with the First Amendment and U.S. Constitution	−0.083 (0.076)	−0.023 (0.052)	−0.187** (0.062)
That dealt with the role of media in society	−0.049 (0.068)	0.082 (0.046)	−0.214*** (0.056)
That dealt primarily with journalism skills	0.269*** (0.071)	0.072 (0.051)	0.245*** (0.064)
Where teacher required reading of newspaper or watching of television news	−0.201* (0.079)	0.006 (0.056)	−0.374*** (0.064)
Extracurricular Activities with News Content			
Student newspaper	0.337** (0.103)	0.093 (0.077)	−0.137 (0.105)
Student magazine	0.069 (0.202)	0.204 (0.161)	0.224 (0.198)
Student radio	1.101*** (0.233)	0.619** (0.208)	0.415 (0.252)
Student television station	−0.036 (0.141)	−0.064 (0.102)	−0.070 (0.132)
Student Internet publication	−0.031 (0.159)	0.026 (0.118)	0.008 (0.153)
Other student news activity	−0.029 (0.153)	−0.253* (0.113)	−0.432** (0.157)
Internet Use and News Consumption			
Use Internet frequently for news	0.035 (0.083)	0.082 (0.057)	−0.603*** (0.074)
Use Internet infrequently for news	−0.073 (0.076)	0.045 (0.051)	−0.380*** (0.062)

(continued)

Table C.3 *(continued)*

	Too Little Freedom	About Right	Don't Know
Use blogs frequently for news	0.335***	0.083	0.118
	(0.089)	(0.063)	(0.080)
Use blogs infrequently for news	0.332***	0.166**	0.135*
	(0.075)	(0.051)	(0.066)
Use chat rooms frequently	0.111	0.028	−0.049
	(0.081)	(0.053)	(0.067)
Use chat rooms infrequently	0.262***	0.086	−0.010
	(0.079)	(0.054)	(0.068)
Blog frequently	0.321***	0.002	−0.135
	(0.089)	(0.063)	(0.081)
Blog infrequently	0.228**	0.168**	0.005
	(0.077)	(0.053)	(0.068)
Demographics and Other Characteristics			
Female	−0.288***	0.029	0.204***
	(0.062)	(0.042)	(0.053)
Hispanic	0.335***	0.097	−0.003
	(0.095)	(0.071)	(0.089)
African American	0.259**	0.021	0.302***
	(0.100)	(0.074)	(0.084)
Asian American	−0.217	−0.087	0.049
	(0.190)	(0.123)	(0.160)
Other race/ethnicity	0.280*	−0.098	0.265*
	(0.134)	(0.102)	(0.117)
U.S. citizen	−0.232	0.179	−0.184
	(0.153)	(0.125)	(0.138)
Economic class—upper income	0.699***	−0.078	0.310*
	(0.143)	(0.123)	(0.138)
Economic class—middle income	0.103	0.053	−0.097
	(0.074)	(0.049)	(0.066)
Economic class—lower income	0.189	0.015	0.050
	(0.106)	(0.076)	(0.092)
Economic class—poor	0.393*	−0.138	0.475**
	(0.191)	(0.156)	(0.154)
Economic class—missing	0.045	−0.051	0.027
	(0.225)	(0.154)	(0.186)
Internet access at home	−0.301***	0.079	0.028
	(0.090)	(0.068)	(0.078)

Table C.3 *(continued)*

	Too Little Freedom	About Right	Don't Know
Internet access at school	−0.551***	−0.100	−0.306**
	(0.110)	(0.090)	(0.100)
Secular private school	0.096	0.197	0.334
	(0.368)	(0.293)	(0.308)
Religious private school	−0.130	0.004	−0.207*
	(0.108)	(0.070)	(0.098)
Self-reported GPA—B	0.211**	0.014	0.366***
	(0.075)	(0.047)	(0.065)
Self-reported GPA—C	0.537***	0.070	0.790***
	(0.090)	(0.062)	(0.077)
Self-reported GPA—D	0.548**	−0.147	0.735***
	(0.171)	(0.139)	(0.145)
Self-reported GPA—F	0.400	−0.069	1.164***
	(0.288)	(0.245)	(0.230)
Self-reported GPA missing	−1.347**	0.043	−2.403***
	(0.430)	(0.335)	(0.353)
10th grader	0.052	−0.017	0.004
	(0.082)	(0.055)	(0.068)
11th grader	0.045	−0.087	−0.035
	(0.086)	(0.059)	(0.074)
12th grader	0.283**	0.007	−0.017
	(0.095)	(0.066)	(0.085)
Constant	−0.590**	−0.088	0.187
	(0.220)	(0.174)	(0.197)
Sample size			14,389

Source: Author's tabulations from FOFA 2006.

Note: Robust standard errors are in parentheses; all standard errors have been adjusted for heteroscedasticity: * significant at 10 percent; ** significant at 5 percent; *** significant at 1 percent.

Table C.4
**Americans Don't Appreciate the First Amendment Freedoms the
Way They Ought To (Q18). Base Group: Agree. Multinomial Logit Results.**

	Disagree	No Opinion
Curriculum and Courses		
Taken class in high school:	(1)	(2)
That dealt with the First Amendment and U.S. Constitution	−0.043	−0.360***
	(0.052)	(0.052)
That dealt with the role of media in society	−0.049	−0.166***
	(0.046)	(0.048)
That dealt primarily with journalism skills	−0.039	0.050
	(0.051)	(0.054)
Where teacher required reading of newspaper or watching of television news	−0.036	−0.126*
	(0.055)	(0.055)
Extracurricular Activities with News Content		
Student newspaper	−0.178*	−0.276**
	(0.078)	(0.086)
Student magazine	0.418**	0.344*
	(0.148)	(0.166)
Student radio	0.008	−0.384*
	(0.166)	(0.193)
Student television station	0.075	0.053
	(0.102)	(0.110)
Student Internet publication	−0.046	0.071
	(0.120)	(0.129)
Other student news activity	−0.086	−0.218
	(0.116)	(0.131)
Internet Use and News Consumption		
Use Internet frequently for news	−0.203***	−0.618***
	(0.058)	(0.062)
Use Internet infrequently for news	−0.059	−0.314***
	(0.052)	(0.052)
Use blogs frequently for news	0.020	−0.063
	(0.063)	(0.069)
Use blogs infrequently for news	0.068	−0.094
	(0.051)	(0.056)
Use chat rooms frequently	0.070	−0.002
	(0.055)	(0.057)

Table C.4 *(continued)*

	Disagree	No Opinion
Use chat rooms infrequently	0.085	−0.058
	(0.054)	(0.058)
Blog frequently	−0.007	−0.227**
	(0.064)	(0.070)
Blog infrequently	0.033	−0.143*
	(0.053)	(0.057)
Demographics and Other Characteristics		
Female	−0.035	0.203***
	(0.042)	(0.045)
Hispanic	0.200**	−0.022
	(0.068)	(0.075)
African American	0.338***	0.340***
	(0.071)	(0.073)
Asian American	0.208	0.216
	(0.125)	(0.134)
Other race/ethnicity	0.305**	0.317**
	(0.098)	(0.102)
U.S. citizen	−0.002	−0.103
	(0.119)	(0.120)
Economic class—upper income	0.045	0.419***
	(0.117)	(0.115)
Economic class—middle income	−0.007	−0.127*
	(0.050)	(0.055)
Economic class—lower income	−0.107	0.028
	(0.077)	(0.078)
Economic class—poor	0.154	0.556***
	(0.147)	(0.134)
Economic class—missing	0.303	0.244
	(0.155)	(0.163)
Internet access at home	−0.125	0.078
	(0.065)	(0.067)
Internet access at school	−0.106	−0.011
	(0.081)	(0.086)
Secular private school	0.422	0.650*
	(0.262)	(0.258)
Religious private school	0.241***	0.008
	(0.070)	(0.081)

(continued)

Table C.4 *(continued)*

	Disagree	No Opinion
Self-reported GPA—B	0.170***	0.288***
	(0.050)	(0.055)
Self-reported GPA—C	0.321***	0.632***
	(0.062)	(0.065)
Self-reported GPA—D	0.298*	0.868***
	(0.135)	(0.125)
Self-reported GPA—F	0.457*	0.927***
	(0.211)	(0.195)
Self-reported GPA missing	−1.212***	−2.123***
	(0.314)	(0.299)
10th grader	−0.038	−0.044
	(0.056)	(0.057)
11th grader	−0.067	−0.200**
	(0.060)	(0.063)
12th grader	0.003	−0.345***
	(0.066)	(0.073)
Constant	−0.675***	−0.338*
	(0.166)	(0.170)
Sample size		14,418

Source: Author's tabulations from FOFA 2006.

Note: Robust standard errors are in parentheses; all standard errors have been adjusted for heteroscedasticity: * significant at 10 percent; ** significant at 5 percent; *** significant at 1 percent.

Table C.5
Rights Guaranteed by the First Amendment (Q19). Base Group:
Personally Think about. Multinomial Logit Results.

	Take for Granted	Don't Know
Curriculum and Courses		
Taken class in high school:	(1)	(2)
That dealt with the First Amendment and U.S.		
Constitution	−0.112*	−0.347***
	(0.057)	(0.058)
That dealt with the role of media in society	−0.152**	−0.328***
	(0.050)	(0.052)
That dealt primarily with journalism skills	−0.207***	0.008
	(0.052)	(0.056)
Where teacher required reading of newspaper or		
watching of television news	−0.016	−0.106
	(0.060)	(0.062)
Extracurricular Activities with News Content		
Student newspaper	0.083	−0.255**
	(0.076)	(0.086)
Student magazine	−0.002	0.128
	(0.158)	(0.168)
Student radio	0.207	−0.350
	(0.170)	(0.195)
Student television station	−0.092	−0.057
	(0.104)	(0.112)
Student Internet publication	−0.017	0.141
	(0.122)	(0.129)
Other student news activity	−0.118	−0.227
	(0.113)	(0.127)
Internet Use and News Consumption		
Use Internet frequently for news	−0.407***	−0.844***
	(0.061)	(0.065)
Use Internet infrequently for news	−0.069	−0.326***
	(0.057)	(0.058)
Use blogs frequently for news	0.189**	0.099
	(0.065)	(0.071)
Use blogs infrequently for news	0.073	−0.011
	(0.054)	(0.058)

(continued)

Table C.5 *(continued)*

	Take for Granted	Don't Know
Use chat rooms frequently	0.027	0.028
	(0.057)	(0.061)
Use chat rooms infrequently	−0.000	−0.016
	(0.057)	(0.061)
Blog frequently	−0.259***	−0.324***
	(0.066)	(0.071)
Blog infrequently	−0.081	−0.155*
	(0.056)	(0.060)
Demographics and Other Characteristics		
Female	−0.064	0.240***
	(0.045)	(0.048)
Hispanic	−0.468***	−0.430***
	(0.071)	(0.075)
African American	−0.397***	−0.047
	(0.077)	(0.076)
Asian American	0.107	0.319*
	(0.137)	(0.148)
Other race/ethnicity	−0.174	0.022
	(0.106)	(0.109)
U.S. citizen	0.046	−0.147
	(0.127)	(0.129)
Economic class—upper income	0.168	0.210
	(0.121)	(0.132)
Economic class—middle income	0.152**	−0.031
	(0.052)	(0.058)
Economic class—lower income	−0.076	−0.090
	(0.080)	(0.083)
Economic class—poor	−0.169	0.291
	(0.163)	(0.152)
Economic class—missing	−0.525**	−0.184
	(0.169)	(0.164)
Internet access at home	0.405***	0.285***
	(0.070)	(0.070)
Internet access at school	0.031	−0.022
	(0.089)	(0.091)
Secular private school	−0.013	0.678*
	(0.311)	(0.280)

Table C.5 *(continued)*

	Take for Granted	Don't Know
Religious private school	0.129	−0.117
	(0.075)	(0.085)
Self-reported GPA—B	−0.076	0.355***
	(0.050)	(0.057)
Self-reported GPA—C	−0.147*	0.652***
	(0.066)	(0.069)
Self-reported GPA—D	0.072	1.011***
	(0.156)	(0.149)
Self-reported GPA—F	0.100	0.813***
	(0.239)	(0.224)
Self-reported GPA missing	0.131	−2.134***
	(0.346)	(0.339)
10th grader	0.022	−0.084
	(0.061)	(0.063)
11th grader	−0.009	−0.314***
	(0.063)	(0.067)
12th grader	0.049	−0.446***
	(0.069)	(0.076)
Constant	0.677***	1.018***
	(0.176)	(0.180)
Sample size		14,360

Source: Author's tabulations from FOFA 2006.

Note: Robust standard errors are in parentheses; all standard errors have been adjusted for heteroscedasticity: * significant at 10 percent; ** significant at 5 percent; *** significant at 1 percent.

Table C.6
**Attitudes toward the First Amendment: People Should
Be Allowed to Express Unpopular Opinions (Q17a).
Base Group: Agree. Multinomial Logit Results.**

	Disagree	No Opinion
Curriculum and Courses		
Taken class in high school:	(1)	(2)
That dealt with the First Amendment and		
U.S. Constitution	−0.172*	−0.185*
	(0.080)	(0.078)
That dealt with the role of media in society	−0.269***	−0.446***
	(0.074)	(0.072)
That dealt primarily with journalism skills	0.296***	0.201*
	(0.081)	(0.082)
Where teacher required reading of newspaper or		
watching of television news	−0.214**	−0.414***
	(0.082)	(0.076)
Extracurricular Activities with News Content		
Student newspaper	−0.073	−0.171
	(0.131)	(0.143)
Student magazine	0.139	0.346
	(0.243)	(0.250)
Student radio	0.115	0.079
	(0.246)	(0.260)
Student television station	0.132	0.125
	(0.161)	(0.166)
Student Internet publication	0.357*	−0.333
	(0.174)	(0.227)
Other student news activity	−0.020	−0.745**
	(0.202)	(0.257)
Internet Use and News Consumption		
Use Internet frequently for news	−0.308**	−0.837***
	(0.097)	(0.101)
Use Internet infrequently for news	−0.145	−0.457***
	(0.083)	(0.077)
Use blogs frequently for news	−0.051	0.017
	(0.107)	(0.110)
Use blogs infrequently for news	0.116	0.053
	(0.083)	(0.087)

Table C.6 *(continued)*

	Disagree	No Opinion
Use chat rooms frequently	−0.311***	−0.270**
	(0.091)	(0.088)
Use chat rooms infrequently	−0.048	−0.311***
	(0.088)	(0.089)
Blog frequently	−0.123	−0.342**
	(0.107)	(0.109)
Blog infrequently	−0.089	−0.332***
	(0.087)	(0.091)
Demographics and Other Characteristics		
Female	−0.187**	−0.081
	(0.070)	(0.068)
Hispanic	0.179	0.034
	(0.108)	(0.109)
African American	0.235*	0.128
	(0.107)	(0.106)
Asian American	0.566**	0.174
	(0.177)	(0.210)
Other race/ethnicity	−0.106	0.238
	(0.169)	(0.141)
U.S. citizen	−0.478**	−0.415**
	(0.154)	(0.158)
Economic class—upper income	0.031	0.604***
	(0.186)	(0.154)
Economic class—middle income	0.156	−0.137
	(0.082)	(0.091)
Economic class—lower income	−0.183	−0.187
	(0.130)	(0.122)
Economic class—poor	0.339	0.607***
	(0.194)	(0.161)
Economic class—missing	0.248	0.451*
	(0.228)	(0.203)
Internet access at home	−0.001	−0.054
	(0.100)	(0.091)
Internet access at school	−0.254*	−0.379***
	(0.119)	(0.107)
Secular private school	0.326	0.427
	(0.347)	(0.292)

(continued)

Table C.6 *(continued)*

	Disagree	No Opinion
Religious private school	−0.486***	−0.904***
	(0.143)	(0.174)
Self-reported GPA—B	0.274**	0.337***
	(0.088)	(0.092)
Self-reported GPA—C	0.544***	0.711***
	(0.103)	(0.101)
Self-reported GPA—D	0.383	0.867***
	(0.197)	(0.165)
Self-reported GPA—F	0.544*	0.768***
	(0.268)	(0.228)
Self-reported GPA missing	−1.565***	−2.221***
	(0.454)	(0.408)
10th grader	0.079	0.030
	(0.087)	(0.085)
11th grader	−0.104	−0.183
	(0.096)	(0.099)
12th grader	−0.288*	−0.155
	(0.115)	(0.114)
Constant	−1.425***	−0.659**
	(0.236)	(0.228)
Sample size		14,392

Source: Author's tabulations from FOFA 2006.

Note: Robust standard errors are in parentheses; all standard errors have been adjusted for heteroscedasticity: * significant at 10 percent; ** significant at 5 percent; *** significant at 1 percent.

Table C.7
Attitudes toward the First Amendment: People Should Be
Allowed to Burn or Deface the American Flag as a Political Statement
(Q17b). Base Group: Agree. Multinomial Logit Results.

	Disagree	No Opinion
Curriculum and Courses		
Taken class in high school:	(1)	(2)
That dealt with the First Amendment and		
U.S. Constitution	0.006	−0.273**
	(0.061)	(0.090)
That dealt with the role of media in society	−0.082	−0.266**
	(0.054)	(0.081)
That dealt primarily with journalism skills	0.023	0.051
	(0.057)	(0.090)
Where teacher required reading of newspaper or		
watching of television news	0.088	−0.196*
	(0.064)	(0.090)
Extracurricular Activities with News Content		
Student newspaper	−0.411***	−0.481***
	(0.080)	(0.140)
Student magazine	−0.172	0.024
	(0.152)	(0.229)
Student radio	−0.978***	−0.904***
	(0.165)	(0.268)
Student television station	0.037	0.255
	(0.111)	(0.167)
Student Internet publication	0.016	0.263
	(0.122)	(0.191)
Other student news activity	0.032	−0.226
	(0.125)	(0.209)
Internet Use and News Consumption		
Use Internet frequently for news	−0.228***	−0.586***
	(0.067)	(0.104)
Use Internet infrequently for news	−0.030	−0.279**
	(0.062)	(0.091)
Use blogs frequently for news	0.115	0.116
	(0.071)	(0.117)
Use blogs infrequently for news	0.062	−0.034
	(0.059)	(0.095)

(continued)

Table C.7 *(continued)*

	Disagree	No Opinion
Use chat rooms frequently	−0.042	−0.316**
	(0.063)	(0.099)
Use chat rooms infrequently	−0.039	−0.166
	(0.063)	(0.095)
Blog frequently	−0.588***	−0.547***
	(0.071)	(0.118)
Blog infrequently	−0.326***	−0.398***
	(0.062)	(0.098)
Demographics and Other Characteristics		
Female	0.490***	0.304***
	(0.050)	(0.076)
Hispanic	−0.408***	0.152
	(0.076)	(0.111)
African American	−0.176*	0.280*
	(0.082)	(0.117)
Asian American	−0.327*	0.351
	(0.138)	(0.203)
Other race/ethnicity	−0.363***	0.148
	(0.108)	(0.154)
U.S. citizen	0.420***	−0.075
	(0.121)	(0.164)
Economic class—upper income	−0.848***	−0.165
	(0.110)	(0.164)
Economic class—middle income	−0.104	−0.227*
	(0.059)	(0.097)
Economic class—lower income	−0.213*	−0.223
	(0.086)	(0.131)
Economic class—poor	−0.567***	−0.012
	(0.144)	(0.186)
Economic class—missing	−0.204	−0.143
	(0.174)	(0.260)
Internet access at home	0.101	0.044
	(0.077)	(0.107)
Internet access at school	0.215*	−0.127
	(0.091)	(0.125)
Secular private school	0.337	0.609
	(0.331)	(0.374)
Religious private school	0.060	−0.582***
	(0.083)	(0.158)

Table C.7 *(continued)*

	Disagree	No Opinion
Self-reported GPA—B	0.023	0.275**
	(0.058)	(0.097)
Self-reported GPA—C	−0.007	0.471***
	(0.071)	(0.112)
Self-reported GPA—D	−0.516***	0.325
	(0.137)	(0.188)
Self-reported GPA—F	−0.550**	0.361
	(0.197)	(0.248)
Self-reported GPA missing	0.713*	−1.031*
	(0.315)	(0.441)
10th grader	−0.116	−0.059
	(0.069)	(0.102)
11th grader	−0.449***	−0.270*
	(0.069)	(0.107)
12th grader	−0.584***	−0.513***
	(0.076)	(0.124)
Constant	1.474***	0.475
	(0.179)	(0.250)
Sample size		14,357

Source: Author's tabulations from FOFA 2006.

Note: Robust standard errors are in parentheses; all standard errors have been adjusted for heteroscedasticity: * significant at 10 percent; ** significant at 5 percent; *** significant at 1 percent.

Table C.8
**Attitudes toward the First Amendment: Musicians Should Be
Allowed to Sing Songs with Lyrics That Others Might Find Offensive
(Q17c). Base Group: Agree. Multinomial Logit Results.**

	Disagree	No Opinion
Curriculum and Courses		
Taken class in high school:	(1)	(2)
That dealt with the First Amendment and		
U.S. Constitution	0.014	−0.234**
	(0.051)	(0.076)
That dealt with the role of media in society	−0.118*	−0.361***
	(0.046)	(0.071)
That dealt primarily with journalism skills	0.142**	0.208*
	(0.050)	(0.081)
Where teacher required reading of newspaper or		
watching of television news	−0.182***	−0.434***
	(0.054)	(0.075)
Extracurricular Activities with News Content		
Student newspaper	−0.170*	−0.266
	(0.079)	(0.136)
Student magazine	0.139	0.329
	(0.153)	(0.232)
Student radio	0.154	−0.017
	(0.177)	(0.267)
Student television station	−0.103	0.093
	(0.105)	(0.162)
Student Internet publication	0.276*	−0.120
	(0.113)	(0.210)
Other student news activity	0.094	−0.248
	(0.113)	(0.210)
Internet Use and News Consumption		
Use Internet frequently for news	−0.060	−0.666***
	(0.059)	(0.098)
Use Internet infrequently for news	0.039	−0.276***
	(0.051)	(0.075)
Use blogs frequently for news	0.027	0.191
	(0.064)	(0.109)
Use blogs infrequently for news	0.148**	0.202*
	(0.051)	(0.083)

Table C.8 *(continued)*

	Disagree	No Opinion
Use chat rooms frequently	−0.184***	−0.363***
	(0.054)	(0.088)
Use chat rooms infrequently	−0.112*	−0.222**
	(0.053)	(0.084)
Blog frequently	−0.292***	−0.546***
	(0.064)	(0.113)
Blog infrequently	−0.202***	−0.300***
	(0.053)	(0.087)
Demographics and Other Characteristics		
Female	0.526***	0.258***
	(0.043)	(0.067)
Hispanic	0.425***	0.230*
	(0.065)	(0.106)
African American	0.313***	0.337**
	(0.069)	(0.104)
Asian American	0.600***	0.892***
	(0.118)	(0.175)
Other race/ethnicity	−0.128	0.209
	(0.106)	(0.143)
U.S. citizen	−0.404***	−0.318*
	(0.108)	(0.159)
Economic class—upper income	−0.121	0.448**
	(0.120)	(0.155)
Economic class—middle income	−0.063	−0.149
	(0.051)	(0.088)
Economic class—lower income	−0.034	−0.187
	(0.075)	(0.120)
Economic class—poor	−0.275	0.300
	(0.154)	(0.167)
Economic class—missing	0.098	0.520*
	(0.156)	(0.208)
Internet access at home	−0.207***	−0.134
	(0.062)	(0.090)
Internet access at school	−0.386***	−0.438***
	(0.080)	(0.108)
Secular private school	−0.397	0.209
	(0.260)	(0.310)

(continued)

Appendix C

Table C.8 *(continued)*

	Disagree	No Opinion
Religious private school	−0.176*	−0.640***
	(0.076)	(0.148)
Self-reported GPA—B	−0.039	0.133
	(0.049)	(0.086)
Self-reported GPA—C	−0.097	0.378***
	(0.062)	(0.099)
Self-reported GPA—D	−0.309*	0.531**
	(0.137)	(0.166)
Self-reported GPA—F	−0.377	0.298
	(0.216)	(0.234)
Self-reported GPA missing	0.717*	−1.067**
	(0.313)	(0.406)
10th grader	−0.076	−0.051
	(0.054)	(0.085)
11th grader	−0.322***	−0.199*
	(0.059)	(0.095)
12th grader	−0.398***	−0.192
	(0.068)	(0.110)
Constant	0.064	−0.464*
	(0.157)	(0.225)
Sample size		14,315

Source: Author's tabulations from FOFA 2006.

Note: Robust standard errors are in parentheses; all standard errors have been adjusted for heteroscedasticity: * significant at 10 percent; ** significant at 5 percent; *** significant at 1 percent.

Table C.9
Attitudes toward the First Amendment: Newspapers Should Be Allowed to Publish Freely without Government Approval of a Story (Q17d). Base Group: Agree. Multinomial Logit Results.

	Disagree	No Opinion
Curriculum and Courses		
Taken class in high school:	(1)	(2)
That dealt with the First Amendment and		
U.S. Constitution	0.089	−0.229***
	(0.047)	(0.069)
That dealt with the role of media in society	−0.027	−0.368***
	(0.041)	(0.065)
That dealt primarily with journalism skills	0.024	0.281***
	(0.046)	(0.071)
Where teacher required reading of newspaper or		
watching of television news	−0.085	−0.363***
	(0.049)	(0.070)
Extracurricular Activities with News Content		
Student newspaper	−0.329***	−0.457***
	(0.070)	(0.126)
Student magazine	0.017	0.282
	(0.145)	(0.218)
Student radio	0.187	0.324
	(0.164)	(0.236)
Student television station	−0.148	0.001
	(0.094)	(0.150)
Student Internet publication	0.201	0.286
	(0.107)	(0.169)
Other student news activity	0.032	−0.237
	(0.104)	(0.182)
Internet Use and News Consumption		
Use Internet frequently for news	−0.258***	−0.867***
	(0.052)	(0.088)
Use Internet infrequently for news	−0.038	−0.384***
	(0.046)	(0.068)
Use blogs frequently for news	0.119*	0.148
	(0.056)	(0.097)
Use blogs infrequently for news	0.021	0.063
	(0.046)	(0.075)

(continued)

Table C.9 *(continued)*

	Disagree	No Opinion
Use chat rooms frequently	0.007	−0.057
	(0.048)	(0.078)
Use chat rooms infrequently	−0.083	−0.143
	(0.049)	(0.078)
Blog frequently	−0.307***	−0.506***
	(0.057)	(0.097)
Blog infrequently	−0.191***	−0.401***
	(0.048)	(0.079)
Demographics and Other Characteristics		
Female	0.456***	0.336***
	(0.038)	(0.061)
Hispanic	−0.045	−0.002
	(0.064)	(0.098)
African American	0.202**	0.171
	(0.064)	(0.096)
Asian American	−0.131	0.233
	(0.117)	(0.178)
Other race/ethnicity	0.064	−0.009
	(0.089)	(0.136)
U.S. citizen	−0.075	−0.228
	(0.108)	(0.150)
Economic class—upper income	−0.237*	0.328*
	(0.109)	(0.143)
Economic class—middle income	−0.053	−0.159*
	(0.045)	(0.078)
Economic class—lower income	−0.115	−0.248*
	(0.068)	(0.109)
Economic class—poor	−0.098	0.615***
	(0.137)	(0.152)
Economic class—missing	0.295*	0.063
	(0.136)	(0.218)
Internet access at home	−0.046	−0.018
	(0.059)	(0.086)
Internet access at school	−0.167*	−0.237*
	(0.076)	(0.105)
Secular private school	−0.487	−0.200
	(0.251)	(0.310)
Religious private school	−0.145*	−0.340**
	(0.066)	(0.119)

Table C.9 *(continued)*

	Disagree	No Opinion
Self-reported GPA—B	0.113*	0.274***
	(0.044)	(0.078)
Self-reported GPA—C	0.157**	0.608***
	(0.056)	(0.088)
Self-reported GPA—D	−0.069	0.560***
	(0.121)	(0.159)
Self-reported GPA—F	−0.158	0.462*
	(0.197)	(0.228)
Self-reported GPA missing	0.011	−1.168**
	(0.284)	(0.376)
10th grader	−0.143**	0.049
	(0.050)	(0.077)
11th grader	−0.154**	−0.019
	(0.053)	(0.085)
12th grader	−0.282***	−0.184
	(0.059)	(0.100)
Constant	−0.060	−0.477*
	(0.152)	(0.214)
Sample size		14,309

Source: Author's tabulations from FOFA 2006.

Note: Robust standard errors are in parentheses; all standard errors have been adjusted for heteroscedasticity: * significant at 10 percent; ** significant at 5 percent; *** significant at 1 percent.

Table C.10
Attitudes toward the First Amendment: High School Students
Should Be Allowed to Report Controversial Issues in Their Student
Newspapers without the Approval of School Authorities (Q17e).
Base Group: Agree. Multinomial Logit Results.

	Disagree	No Opinion
Curriculum and Courses		
Taken class in high school:	(1)	(2)
That dealt with the First Amendment and		
U.S. Constitution	0.157**	−0.140*
	(0.051)	(0.067)
That dealt with the role of media in society	−0.090*	−0.390***
	(0.045)	(0.062)
That dealt primarily with journalism skills	0.132**	0.174*
	(0.049)	(0.071)
Where teacher required reading of newspaper or		
watching of television news	−0.094	−0.366***
	(0.053)	(0.067)
Extracurricular Activities with News Content		
Student newspaper	−0.287***	−0.265*
	(0.078)	(0.118)
Student magazine	0.089	0.291
	(0.157)	(0.214)
Student radio	0.381*	0.230
	(0.172)	(0.224)
Student television station	−0.170	−0.232
	(0.105)	(0.149)
Student Internet publication	0.189	0.345*
	(0.116)	(0.162)
Other student news activity	−0.170	−0.485*
	(0.116)	(0.188)
Internet Use and News Consumption		
Use Internet frequently for news	−0.224***	−0.782***
	(0.056)	(0.085)
Use Internet infrequently for news	−0.070	−0.336***
	(0.049)	(0.066)
Use blogs frequently for news	−0.010	0.026
	(0.062)	(0.094)

Table C.10 *(continued)*

	Disagree	No Opinion
Use blogs infrequently for news	0.091	0.087
	(0.050)	(0.072)
Use chat rooms frequently	−0.097	−0.120
	(0.052)	(0.076)
Use chat rooms infrequently	−0.080	−0.131
	(0.053)	(0.075)
Blog frequently	−0.257***	−0.426***
	(0.063)	(0.094)
Blog infrequently	−0.169**	−0.299***
	(0.052)	(0.076)
Demographics and Other Characteristics		
Female	0.382***	0.021
	(0.041)	(0.058)
Hispanic	−0.206**	−0.152
	(0.070)	(0.092)
African American	−0.010	0.040
	(0.070)	(0.093)
Asian American	−0.079	0.053
	(0.127)	(0.180)
Other race/ethnicity	−0.130	−0.022
	(0.100)	(0.128)
U.S. citizen	−0.341**	−0.565***
	(0.116)	(0.137)
Economic class—upper income	−0.268*	0.423**
	(0.122)	(0.133)
Economic class—middle income	−0.101*	−0.119
	(0.049)	(0.074)
Economic class—lower income	−0.076	−0.132
	(0.074)	(0.102)
Economic class—poor	−0.302	0.528***
	(0.155)	(0.146)
Economic class—missing	0.253	−0.082
	(0.141)	(0.212)
Internet access at home	−0.027	−0.068
	(0.064)	(0.081)
Internet access at school	−0.004	−0.316**
	(0.082)	(0.096)

(continued)

Table C.10 *(continued)*

	Disagree	No Opinion
Secular private school	0.226	−0.083
	(0.246)	(0.331)
Religious private school	−0.106	−0.255*
	(0.073)	(0.113)
Self-reported GPA—B	−0.086	0.278***
	(0.047)	(0.076)
Self-reported GPA—C	−0.025	0.601***
	(0.060)	(0.086)
Self-reported GPA—D	−0.192	0.886***
	(0.136)	(0.142)
Self-reported GPA—F	−0.136	0.501*
	(0.214)	(0.216)
Self-reported GPA missing	0.215	−1.777***
	(0.310)	(0.359)
10th grader	−0.049	−0.092
	(0.054)	(0.074)
11th grader	−0.160**	−0.132
	(0.058)	(0.080)
12th grader	−0.254***	−0.413***
	(0.065)	(0.099)
Constant	−0.324*	0.040
	(0.163)	(0.197)
Sample size		14,379

Source: Author's tabulations from FOFA 2006.

Note: Robust standard errors are in parentheses; all standard errors have been adjusted for heteroscedasticity: * significant at 10 percent; ** significant at 5 percent; *** significant at 1 percent.

Selected Bibliography

Books

Adams, Charles Francis, ed. 1851. *The works of John Adams*. Boston: Little & Brown.

Chun, Wendy, and Thomas Keenan, eds. 2003. *New media, old media: Interrogating the digital revolution*. New York: Routledge.

Easton, David. 1965. *A systems analysis of political life*. New York: Wiley & Sons.

Easton, David, and Jack Dennis. 1969. *Children in the political system: Origins of political legitimacy*. New York: McGraw-Hill.

Erikson, Robert, and Kent Tedin. 2001. *American public opinion*. New York: Longman.

Fuhrman, Susan, and Marvin Lazerson, eds. 2005. *American institutions of democracy: The public schools*. New York: Oxford University Press.

Gimpel, James, J. Celeste Lay, and Jason E. Schuknecht. 2003. *Cultivating democracy: Civic environments and political socialization in America*. Washington, D.C.: Brookings Institution Press.

Harrow, Robert. 2005. *No place to hide: Behind the scenes of our emerging surveillance society*. New York: Free Press.

Haynes, Charles C., Sam Chaltain, John Ferguson, and David L. Hudson Jr. 2003. *The First Amendment in schools: A guide from the First Amendment Center*. Nashville, TN: The First Amendment Center.

Hewitt, Hugh. 2005. *Blog: Understanding the information reformation that's changing your world*. Nashville, TN: Thomas Nelson, Inc.

Hochschild, Jennifer, and Nathan Scovronick. 2003. *The American dream and the public schools*. New York: Oxford University Press.

Howe, Neil, William Strauss, and R. J. Matson. 2000. *Millennials rising: The next generation*. New York: Vintage.

Key, V. O. 1963. *Public opinion and American democracy*. New York: Alfred A. Knopf.

Lancaster, Lynne, and David Stillman. 2003. *When generations collide: Who they are. Why they clash. How to solve the generational problem at work.* New York: Collins.

Levy, Leonard. 1985. *The emergence of a free press.* New York: Oxford University Press.

Macedo, Stephen, ed. 2005. *Democracy at risk: How political choices undermine citizen participation and what we can do about it.* Washington D.C.: Brookings Institution Press.

McCloskey, Herbert, and Alida Brill. 1983. *Dimensions of tolerance: What Americans believe about civil liberties.* New York: Russell Sage Foundation.

McCormick Tribune Foundation. 2007. *Free speech 3.0: Student expression in a digital age.* Chicago, IL: McCormick Tribune Foundation.

McDonnell, Lorraine M., P. Michael Timpane, and Roger Benjamin, eds. 2000. *Rediscovering the democratic purposes of education.* Lawrence: University Press of Kansas.

Merelman, Richard. 1971. *Political socialization and educational climates.* New York: Holt & Co.

——. 1984. *Making something of ourselves: On culture and politics in the United States.* Berkeley: University of California Press.

Milner, Henry. 2002. *Civic literacy: How informed citizens make democracy work.* Hanover, NH: University Press of New England.

Mindich, David T. Z. 2005. *Tuned out: Why Americans under 40 don't follow the news.* New York: Oxford University Press.

Overholser, Geneva, and Kathleen Hall Jamison, eds. 2005. *American institutions of American democracy: The press.* New York: Oxford University Press.

Reynolds, Glenn. 2006. *An army of Davids: How markets and technology empower ordinary people to beat big media, big government and other Goliaths.* Nashville, TN: Nelson Current.

Skocpol, Theda, and Morris P. Fiorina, eds. 1999. *Civic engagement in American democracy.* Washington D.C.: Brookings Institution Press.

Stouffer, Samuel. 1955. *Communism, conformity and civil liberties.* New York: Doubleday.

Yalof, David, and Kenneth Dautrich. 2002. *The First Amendment and the media in the court of public opinion.* Cambridge: Cambridge University Press.

Articles

Avery, Patricia, Karen Bird, Sondra Johnstone, John L. Sullivan, and Kristina Thalhammer. 1991. "Exploring political tolerance." *Theory and Research in Social Education* 20: 386–420.

Beder, Michael. 2006. "Free speech fight hits Kirkwood High." *St. Louis Post-Dispatch,* May 24, p. A1.

Cassidy, John. 2006. "Me media: How hanging out on the Internet became big business." *New Yorker,* May 15, 50–59.

Dvorak, Jack. 1998. "Journalism performance on Advanced Placement exams." *Journalism and Mass Communication Educator* 53: 4–12.

Eccles, Jacquelynne A., and Bonnie Barber. 1999. "Student council, volunteering, basketball or marching band: What kind of extracurricular involvement matters?" *Journal of Adolescent Research* 14: 10–43.

Goldenson, Dennis. 1978. "An alternative view about the role of secondary schools in political socialization: A field-experimental study of the development of civil liberties attitudes." *Theory and Research in Social Education* 6: 386–420.

Jennings, M. Kent, and Richard Niemi. 1975. "Continuity and change in political orientations: A longitudinal study of two generations." *American Political Science Review* 69: 1316–35.

Kornblum, Jack. 2006. "Teens hang out at MySpace." USAToday.com, July 12 (accessed 1 March 2008).

Langton, Kenneth, and M. Kent Jennings. 1968. "Political socialization and the high school civics curriculum in the United States." *American Political Science Review* 62: 852–67.

Lemann, Nicholas. 2006. "The wayward press: Amateur hour." *New Yorker*, August 7 and 14, 44.

Lipka, Sara. 2006. "Stopping the presses." *Chronicle of Higher Education*, March 3, A35–A36.

Mahoney, Joseph. 2000. "School extracurricular activity participation as a moderator in the development of antisocial patterns." *Child Development* 71: 502–16.

Mahoney, Joseph, and Robert Cairns. 1991. "Do extracurricular activities protect against early school dropout?" *Developmental Psychology* 33: 241–53.

Marsh, Herbert W. 1991. "Extracurricular activities: Beneficial extension of the traditional curriculum or subversion of academic goals?" *Journal of Educational Psychology* 84: 553–62.

McNeal, Ralph B. "Extracurricular activities and high school dropouts." *Sociology of Education* 68: 62–81.

McPhillips, Dorothy. 1998. "ACT research report validates journalism in the curriculum." *NASSP Bulletin* 72: 11–16.

Merelman, Richard. 1971. "The development of policy thinking in adolescence." *American Political Science Review* 64: 1033–47.

———. 1980. "Democratic politics and the culture of American education." *American Political Science Review* 61: 751–58.

Prothro, J., and C. Grigg. 1960. "Fundamental principles of democracy: Bases of agreement and disagreement." *Journal of Politics* 22: 276–94.

Ramasastry, Anita. 2006. "Can schools punish students for posting offensive content on MySpace and similar sites?" *Modern Practice*, May 4 at http://practice.findlaw.com/ramasastry/20060501.html (accessed July 14, 2006).

Read, Brock, and Jeffrey R. Young. 2006. "Facebook and other social-networking sites raise questions for administrators." *Chronicle of Higher Education*, August 4, A29.

Saavedra, Sherry. 2006. "How much space to give MySpace users?" *San Diego Union Tribune*, June 4 at www.signonsandiego.com/uniontrib/20060604/news_1in4myspace.html (accessed 1 March 2008).

Sears, David O., and Nicholas Valentino. 1997. "Politics matters: Political events as catalysts for pre-adult socialization." *American Political Science Review* 91: 45–64.
Sears, David O., and Nicholas Valentino. 1997. "Politics matters: Political events as catalysts for pre-adult socialization." *American Political Science Review* 91: 45–64.
Student Press Law Center. 1992. "*Hazelwood School District v. Kuhlmeier*: A complete guide to the Supreme Court decision." Student Press Law Center Website, www.splc.org/legalresearch.asp?id=4 (accessed July 16, 2006).

Main Survey Research Consulted

Freedom Forum State of the First Amendment Survey 1997 ("SOFA 1997")
Freedom Forum State of the First Amendment Survey 1999 ("SOFA 1999")
Freedom Forum State of the First Amendment Survey 2000 ("SOFA 2000")
Freedom Forum State of the First Amendment Survey 2001 ("SOFA 2001")
Freedom Forum State of the First Amendment Survey 2002 ("SOFA 2002")
Freedom Forum State of the First Amendment Survey 2003 ("SOFA 2003")
Freedom Forum State of the First Amendment Survey 2004 ("SOFA 2004")
Freedom Forum State of the First Amendment Survey 2005 ("SOFA 2005")
Knight Foundation Future of the First Amendment Study 2004 ("FOFA 2004")
Knight Foundation Future of the First Amendment Study 2006 ("FOFA 2006")
Pew Internet & American Life Project: Parents & Teens Survey 2004.
Pew Internet & American Life Project: Parents & Teens Survey 2006.

Index

About the Authors

Kenneth Dautrich is professor in the Department of Public Policy at the University of Connecticut. He is author of *American Government: Historical, Popular, and Global Perspectives* (2008), *The First Amendment and the Media in the Court of Public Opinion* (2002), and *How the News Media Fail the American Voter* (1999), as well as many other books, articles, and book chapters on elections, public opinion, and voting. He is founder and former director of the Center for Survey Research and Analysis at the University of Connecticut, and has been a senior research fellow at the Heldrich Center for Workforce Development (Rutgers University) and a research fellow at the Media Studies Center (Columbia University and the Freedom Forum). He established the Masters in Survey Research degree program as the University of Connecticut and teaches courses in survey research and polling. He has directed a number of national polls on voting in presidential elections, including a series of polls for TIME Magazine on the 2004 and 2008 presidential elections. He directs an annual survey on the "State of the First Amendment" for the Freedom Forum's First Amendment Center and has conducted a number of studies on civic literacy for the Intercollegiate Studies Institute. His Ph.D. is from Rutgers University.

David A. Yalof received his Ph.D. in political science from Johns Hopkins University and his law degree from the University of Virginia. He is currently an associate professor of political science at the University of Connecticut. His first book, *Pursuit of Justices: Presidential Politics and the Selection of Supreme Court Nominees* (1999), was awarded the American Political Science Association's Richard E. Neustadt Award as the best book published on presidential studies in 1999. He is also the coauthor of *The First Amendment and the Media in the Court of Public Opinion* (2001) and two textbooks, *Civil Liberty and Individual Rights* (2007) and *An Introduction to American Government* (2008). His articles have been published in *Political Research Quarterly, Judicature, Constitutional Commentary,* and other journals.

Mark Hugo López is the associate director of the Pew Hispanic Center. He received his Ph.D. in economics from Princeton University. At the Center, he studies political engagement among Latinos and helps to coordinate the Center's national surveys. Prior to joining the Center, he served as research director at the Center for Information and Research on Civic Learning and Engagement (CIRCLE) at the University of Maryland. Through his work at CIRCLE, he has studied young people's electoral participation, the civic engagement of immigrants, young people's views of the first amendment, and the link between college attendance and civic engagement. In other work, he has studied the earnings differential between U.S.-born Hispanic faculty and other faculty, the impact of bilingual education programs on long-term student achievement, the return to speaking a second language, and the neighborhood effects of immigrants on the educational achievement of natives. He joined the Pew Hispanic Center in January of 2008.